Birmingham Repertory Theatre Company presents

GRAVITY
BY ARZHANG LUKE PEZHMAN

First performed by Birmingham Repertory Theatre Company
at mac in February 2012

Following the play's world premiere at mac the production
tours, supported by the Sir Barry Jackson Trust.

Supported by
THE
SIR BARRY JACKSON
TRUST

T0347972

GRAVITY

BY ARZHANG LUKE PEZHMAN

CAST

(in order of appearance)

DAVID	Nigel Hastings
KATHY	Imogen Slaughter
KYLE	Ashley Hunter
REECE	Boris Mitkov
CHANTAY	Rebecca Loudon

Director	Rae McKen
Designer	Fabrice Serafino
Lighting Designer	Simon Bond
Composer and Sound Designer	Edward Lewis
Casting Director	Alison Solomon
Dramaturg	Kate Chapman
Stage Manager	Paul Southern
Deputy Stage Manager	Andrew McCarthy

CAST

NIGEL HASTINGS
DAVID

Nigel trained at LAMDA.

Theatre credits include: *Journey's End* (Duke of York's West End and tour); *Animal Farm, The Lemon Princess, The Lady In The Van* (West Yorkshire Playhouse); *The Ugly One* (Theatre Royal Norwich); *Amadeus* (Sheffield Crucible); *Othello* (Shakespeare's Globe); *Pravda* (Chichester/ Birmingham Repertory Theatre); *Hamlet, The Seagull, Round Two* (Factory Theatre/Bristol Old Vic); *Present Laughter* (Theatre Royal Bath and tour); *Macbeth, As You Like It* (Sprite); *Hurts Given and Received, Found In The Ground, The Fence* (The Wrestling School); *Gone* (Edinburgh Festival and New Ambassadors West End); *Parting Shots* (Stephen Joseph Theatre, Scarborough); *House & Garden* (Northampton Theatres); *Jerusalem Syndrome* (Soho Theatre); *Kindertransport* (Vaudeville West End); *All My Sons* (Theatre Royal Plymouth); *Twelfth Night* (Edinburgh Lyceum/ Salisbury Playhouse); *The Devils* (Theatr Clwyd); *As You Like It, A Midsummer Night's Dream* (Open Air Theatre Regent's Park); *Pride and Prejudice* (Royal Exchange, Manchester); *Julius Caesar* (Compass Theatre); *Mary Stuart* (Edinburgh International Festival).

Film and Television credits include: *Hanna's War, Four Weddings and a Funeral, Hostage, The Shadow Line, Hustle, Rosemary and Thyme, The Government Inspector, Wire in the Blood, The Commander, A Touch Of Frost, Attachments, McCallum, EastEnders, Soldier Soldier, The Ring, Cadfael, The Big Battalions, Rumpole, Calling the Shots* and *A Bit Of A Do.*

IMOGEN SLAUGHTER
KATHY

Imogen Slaughter trained at The Oxford School of Drama.

Theatre credits include: *The Eden Cinema, Baal, Dr Faustus, Iphigenia, A Midsummer Night's Dream, The Tempest, Speer* (NT); *Look Back In Anger* (NT); *Lulu* (The Almeida Theatre); *Private Fears in Public Places* (The Library Theatre Manchester); *Ordinary Dreams* (The Trafalgar Studios); *Titanic Tales, Baby With The Bathwater, The Merchant of Venice* (The Clerkenwell Theatre Company); *My Cousin Rachel, Far from The Madding Crowd* and *Fiddlers Three* (The Jill Freud Company).

Television credits include: *Sherlock, Silent Witness, Doctors, The Bill, Elizabeth I, Boudica.*

Film credits include: *The Last Temptation of Chris, The Bench, One Careful Owner.*

ASHLEY HUNTER
KYLE

Ashley trained at Central School of Speech and Drama.

Theatre credits include: Alex in *A Clockwork Orange* (Theatre Royal Stratford East).

Theatre credits while training include: *Epsom Downs, All My Sons, King Lear, Romeo And Juliet, Blues For Mister Charlie, The Relapse, The Crucible* and *Twelfth Night*.

Radio credits includes: *One Million Tiny Plays* (BBC Radio 4).

REBECCA LOUDEN
CHANTAY

Rebecca trained at Mountview.

Theatre credits include: *The Malcontent, Romeo and Juliet* (Custom/Practice); *The Black Diamond* (Punchdrunk); *Respect* (Birmingham Repertory Theatre); *Sick Room* (NYT); *20 Cigarettes* (NYT).

Theatre whilst training: *The Seagull, The Winters Tale, Awake and Sing, Nine*.

Films credits include: *Another World* (Lunar Films); *Josephine* (Breathless Productions).

BORIS MITKOV
REECE

Boris trained at Arts Ed.

Theatre credits include: *The Malcontent* (White Bear Theatre).

Theatre credits whilst training: *Roberto Zucco, Romeo and Juliet, Someone Who'll Watch Over Me, The Cherry Orchard, Antigone, Golden Boy, Private Lives, Macbeth* (Arts Ed).

CREATIVE TEAM

ARZHANG LUKE PEZHMAN
WRITER

Theatre credits include: *Local* (Royal Court Theatre, 2000); *Come Around* (part of the Rampage season, Royal Court Theatre, 2003); *Mother's Day* (Wolverhampton Grammar School, 2003); *Tics* (Birmingham Repertory Youth Theatre, 2004); *Blood at the Root* (London Metropolitan University, 2005); *Bolt-Hole* (Birmingham Repertory Theatre, 2006); *Writer-in-Residence at Soho Theatre* (2006); *Intervention* (Birmingham Repertory Theatre, 2008); *Borderland (*Fairfield High School, 2010); *Soul Seekers* (Central Youth Theatre, 2011).

Feature Film Scripts: *Kirigami* (Script/Small Screen Visions/ Claire Ingham, 2002); *Our Home* (Reza Shirazi/Media Art, 2011).

Arzhang also works extensively as a dramaturge and writing tutor. He is currently developing a new play for stage, a six-part television series and a short story for children/teenagers which he also hopes to develop into a stage play.

RAE MCKEN
DIRECTOR

Rae studied for her MA in Text and Performance from King's College London and RADA and with the National Studio Director's programme. She was also a recipient of the Channel 4 Regional Director's Scheme. Rae is Co-Artistic Director of Custom/Practice.

Directing includes: *The Malcontent, Romeo & Juliet, Macbeth* (Custom/Practice); *Respect* (Birmingham Repertory Theatre); *Jamie the Saxt* (Finborough Theatre); *Origin Unkown* (Theatre Royal Stratford East); *Airswimming* (Salisbury Playhouse); *Stamping, Shouting and Singing Home* (*mac* and national tour); and *Women Beware Women* (Landor Theatre).

Associate Director: *The Wiz* (Birmingham Repertory Theatre)

Assistant Directing includes: *Noughts and Crosses* and *Penelopiad* (RSC); *The Snow Queen, The Harder They Come* (Theatre Royal Stratford East); *93.2FM* (Royal Court); *Much Ado About Nothing* (Salisbury Playhouse); *Mother Courage and her Children* (Nottingham Playhouse); and *Simply Heavenly* (The Young Vic).

FABRICE SERAFINO
DESIGNER

Fabrice's theatre experience includes 15 years as a dancer for various internationally renowned companies. In September 2004, he left dancing to attend the prestigious Motley Theatre Design Course. Since then, he has designed extensively for theatre, dance and opera.

Theatre designs include *Or Nearest Offer* (Almeida Theatre); *On the Harmful Effect of Tobacco/Can Cause Death* (Forward Theatre Project, National Theatre); *Macbeth* (Custom/Practice,UK tour); *Medea* (Theatre Royal Stratford East); *POOL(NO WATER)* (Norwich Playhouse); *Little Eyolf* (Jermyn Street Theatre); *Mad Forest* (Cockpit Theatre); *Wild Fruit* (Oval House); *Savage/Love - Motel Chronicles* (Theatre503); *Hitting Town* (Southwark Playhouse); *Maratona de Nova Iorque* (Guimaraes, Portugal); *The Cage, The Grizzled Skipper, Peter Pan, The Story of Aladdin, The Wind in The Willows, Riverside Drive/Old Saybrook, A Christmas Carol, The Borrowers, 20,000 Leagues Under the Sea* (all Nuffield theatre, Southampton).

Dance and opera designs include *Elegie* (Linbury Studio, ROH2); *Nest, In The Hands of Others, Solo?, Anatomica #3* (rambert Dance Company); *Magpie* (Probe, UK tour); *Dear Body* (Protein Dance, UK tour); *Hinterland* (Bare Bones Dance, UK tour); *Kith/ Kin, Gameshow* (Company Chameleon, UK tour); *The Time of our Freedom* (YMT:UK, Belfast); *Krazy Kat, Lite Bites* (Tête à Tête: The Opera Festival).

Visit www.fabriceserafino.com for more details.

SIMON BOND
LIGHTING DESIGNER

Simon is a Lighting Technician at Birmingham Repertory Theatre.

Recent designs include: *Respect, Cling To Me Like Ivy, 8sixteen32, Looking For Yoghurt, Notes To Future Self, The Importance Of Being Earnest* and *Travesties.*

EDWARD LEWIS
COMPOSER AND SOUND DESIGNER

Edward studied Music at Oxford University and subsequently trained as a composer and sound designer at the Bournemouth Media School. He has worked on numerous theatre productions, as well as for film, television and radio.

Recent theatre credits include: *On The Rocks, Amongst Friends* and *Darker Shores* (Hampstead Theatre); *Slowly, Hurts Given and Received* and *Apple Pie* (Riverside Studios); *Measure For Measure* (Cardiff Sherman); *Emo* (Bristol Old Vic and Young

Vic); *Once Upon A Time in Wigan* and *65 Miles* (Paines Plough / Hull Truck Theatre); *I Am Falling* (Sadler's Wells & The Gate, Notting Hill); *Orpheus and Eurydice* and *Quartet* (Old Vic Tunnels); *The Stronger, The Pariah, Boy With A Suitcase, Le Marriage* and *Meetings* (The Arcola); *The Shallow End* (Southwark Playhouse); *Hedda* and *Breathing Irregular* (The Gate, Notting Hill); *Madness In Valencia* (Trafalgar Studios); *The Madness Of George III* and *Macbeth* (National Tours); *Othello* (Rose Theatre, Bankside); *Love, Question Mark* (New Diorama); *Knives In Hens* (Battersea Arts Centre); *Personal Enemy* (White Bear & New York); *Accolade, Rigor Mortis, Fog, Perchance To Dream, Drama At Inish, In The Blood, The December Man, Beating Heart Cadaver, Blue Surge, Portraits* and *Mirror Teeth* (Finborough Theatre); *Kalagora* (National and International Tour); *The Winter's Tale* (Camley Street Nature Reserve / Old Vic Tunnels); *The Sexual Awakening Of Peter Mayo, Mad, Funny, Just* and *Mimi And The Stalker* (Theatre503); *The London Plays* (The Old Red Lion); *Cyrano De Bergerac, The Malcontent, Bloody Poetry, The Winterling* and *Madman's Confession* (White Bear); *No Way Out* (Hen and Chickens); *Not About Heroes* (Lion and Unicorn); *The Pork Crunch* (Pleasance); *Coffin* (King's Head); *Striking 12* (Waterloo East Theatre);

Heat and Light (Hampstead Theatre); *Diary Of A Madman* (The Rosemary Branch); *The Death Of Cool* (Tristan Bates); and *Full Circle* (Oval House), as well as on the Arden Project for the Old Vic and the Vibrant season at the Finborough Theatre. He has recently been nominated for several Off West End Theatre Awards, and films he has recently worked on have won several awards at the LA International Film Festival and Filmstock International Film Festival.

As a trained musician, Edward is fascinated by the relationship between sound design and musical composition, and by the artistic possibilities inherent in their broadening overlap in a live production. He works as both a sound designer and composer in differing styles, believing both traditional and contemporary, and both naturalistic and abstract approaches have their place in different productions. He also works as a conductor and music critic.

edwardjlewis@gmail.com

ALISON SOLOMON
CASTING DIRECTOR

As Casting Director for Birmingham Repertory Theatre: *Mustafa, The Wiz* (Community Cast), *Notes To Future Self, Respect, Behna (Sisters), Grass Routes Festival, East is East* with Sooki McShane as lead Casting Director, *These Four Streets, Looking For Yoghurt* British cast (Birmingham Repertory Theatre, Joyful Theatre and Kijimuna Festa in association with Hanyong Theatre); *Rosetta Life, Toy Theatres, The Speckled Monster* (Birmingham Repertory Theatre in Association with University of Birmingham); *At The Gates of Gaza* (Big Creative Ideas in Association with Birmingham Repertory Theatre); *360 Degrees (GENERATION), TRANSMISSIONS Festival 'The Big 10'.*

Norman Beaton Fellowship 2012, 2011, 2010 & 2008 - BBC Radio Drama (Birmingham) and Birmingham Repertory Theatre.

As Children's Casting Director for Birmingham Repertory Theatre: *A Christmas Carol, The Grapes of Wrath, Orphans, Once On This Island, An Inspector Calls, Hapgood, Peter Pan, Wizard of Oz, Galileo.*

Recent workshops / readings include: *Butcher, I Was A Rat!, Gravity, Shell Shock, Bookface, Mustafa, Transmissions, Without Parade, Our House, Pwnage, Broken Stones, Notes to Future Self, Grass Routes Workshops, Coming Out From the Cold, Fairytale Toy Theatres, Dealing With Dreams, Cling to Me Like Ivy, Respect, Dirty Fingernails, Engaged, After Margritte, In Extremis* and *Handbag.*

BIRMINGHAM REPERTORY THEATRE COMPANY

Administrative Assistant
Richard Harris

Head of Marketing & Communications
Paul Reece

Communications & PR Manager
Clare Jepson-Homer

Marketing & Communications Officer
Eleanor Miles

Digital Officer
Clare Lovell

Development Manager
Anya Sampson

Development Officer
Ros Adams

Development Office
Kayleigh Cottam
(Maternity cover)

REP 100 Archive Researcher
Sara Crathorne

Theatre Manager
Nigel Cairns

Sales Manager
Gerard Swift

Sales Team Supervisor
Rebecca Thorndyke

Sales Development Supervisor
Rachel Foster

Sales Team
Anne Bower
Kayleigh Cottam
Sebastian Maynard-Francis
Eileen Minnock

Stage Door Reception
Tracey Dolby
Robert Flynn

Cleaning by
We Clean Limited

Head of Production
Tomas Wright

Production Manager
Milorad Zakula

Production Assistant
Hayley Seddon

Head of Stage
Adrian Bradley

Head of Lighting
Andrew Fidgeon

Lighting Design Technician
Simon Bond

Head of Sound
Dan Hoole

Deputy Head of Sound
Clive Meldrum

Company Manager
Ruth Morgan

Workshop Supervisor
Margaret Rees

Construction Coordinator
Oliver Shapley

Deputy Workshop Supervisor
Simon Fox

Carpenter/Metalworker
Rachel Denning

Head Scenic Artist
Christopher Tait

Head of Wardrobe
Sue Nightingale

Wardrobe
Liz Vass

Head of Wigs and Make-up
Andrew Whiteoak

With thanks to the following volunteers
Student REPresentatives

REP Archivist
Horace Gillis

_{THE} REP A CHANGE OF SCENERY

Birmingham Repertory Theatre

Birmingham Repertory Theatre is one of Britain's leading producing theatre companies. Founded nearly 100 years ago by Sir Barry Jackson, the company will celebrate its centenary in 2013.

As a pioneer of new plays, the commissioning and production of new work lies at the core of The REP's programme and over the last five years the company has produced more than 130 new plays.

The REP's productions regularly transfer to London and tour nationally and internationally. Recent tours have included: *The Snowman* which made its international debut in Korea in 2009 and performed in Birmingham, Salford, Finland and London in 2011, a new staging of Philip Pullman's *His Dark Materials*, the world premiere of Dennis Kelly's *Orphans*, Simon Stephens' *Pornography*, Lucy Caldwell's *Notes to Future Self*, Samantha Ellis's *Cling To Me Like Ivy, Looking For Yoghurt* – a new play for young children which played at theatres in the UK, Japan and Korea – and *These Four Streets* – a multi-authored play about the 2005 Lozells disturbances.

Developing new and particularly younger audiences is also at the heart of The REP's work. The theatre's Learning and Participation department engages with over 10,000 young people each year through various initiatives including The Young REP, REP's Children, Grass Routes writing programme for 18–30 year olds and the Transmissions Playwriting programme in schools.

The REP is currently undergoing re-development as part of the new Library of Birmingham, which is due to open in 2013. This new partnership will see the two cultural venues sharing public spaces and a new purpose-built 300-seat auditorium. This marks a significant period in the history of The REP and it brings an exciting time artistically as audiences are currently able to enjoy and experience an imaginative programme of REP productions in other theatres and non-theatrical spaces across Birmingham.

The company has also recently announced the appointment of Roxana Silbert as artistic director. Roxana will join The REP for the company's centenary celebrations and return to its newly-developed building in 2013.

Artistic Director (Designate) Roxana Silbert
Executive Director Stuart Rogers

Box Office: 0121 236 4455
Administration: 0121 245 2000
birmingham-rep.co.uk

Birmingham Repertory Theatre is a registered charity, number 223660

Arzhang Luke Pezhman

GRAVITY

OBERON BOOKS
LONDON

WWW.OBERONBOOKS.COM

First published in 2012 by Oberon Books Ltd
521 Caledonian Road, London N7 9RH

A catalogue record for this book is available from the British
Library.

ISBN: 978-1-84943-154-5

Cover image by Indigo River

With thanks to; Caroline Jester, Nisha Modhwadia, Alison Solomon, Raidene Carter and everyone else at the Birmingham Rep over the past ten years, Kate Chapman (Theatre Writing Partnerships) Emily McLaughlin, Ola Animashawun, Aoife Mannix, Nic Wass (Royal Court Theatre), Nina Steiger (Soho Theatre), Claire Ingham (Red Room Films), Jane Ward (Central Youth Theatre), Ian Tyler (W.G.S.), Nick Marston, Camilla Young (Curtis Brown), Rae McKen, Clare Symonds and the Arts Council England, the Peggy Ramsay Foundation, the Writers' Guild, Harun and Laura (Fierce), Christine McGowan (Newhampton Arts Centre), David Edgar, April de Angelis (Birmingham University), Paul Ward (Leeds University), Dymphna Callery, Peter Taylor, Bill Green (Wolverhampton University), Catherine Edwards, Claire Hodgson, Steve Johnstone and everyone at Black Country Touring, Jan and Deb and the rest of the Science department at Northicote school, Maarten Wilbers, Peter Kroon, my gorgeous nephew Kiyan, my beautiful goddaughters Elizabeth Wilcox and Isabella Gough as well as the lovely Charlotte and Poppy Kelly, the friends that have talked and laughed with me every step of the way and my family that have inspired me, scattered across the country and the rest of the world.

For Farhad, Norma and Zal

To Kerry

Characters

DAVID – Science teacher, mid-fifties

KATHY – Senior Management, early forties

KYLE – late developer, fourteen/fifteen

REECE – hard faced, fourteen/fifteen

CHANTAY – distracted, fourteen/fifteen

Notes:

A slash (/) indicates an interruption in speech.

Most scenes require a presence from the rest of the school. Often there is unseen traffic. This should be represented accordingly, depending on location and circumstance.

Fig 1.

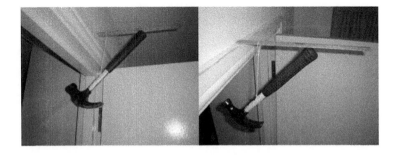

'There was a young lady of Wight,
Who travelled much faster than light,
She departed one day,
In a relative way,
And arrived on the previous night'

Stephen Hawking

SCENE 1

A school science prep room. Chemicals/bottles, weights/levers, plants/microscopes etc. On a central bench there is a piece of string and a hammer. A tub of rulers sit with other stationery further down the bench. DAVID is at the sink, sleeves rolled up, washing his hands. He is unkempt and restless. KATHY enters.

MRS. JONES: David?

DAVID: They've done it Kathy.

MRS. JONES: What's that?

DAVID: They've only gone and done it. Those boys/

MRS. JONES: Which boys?

DAVID: At CERN.

MRS. JONES: Right, those boys.

DAVID dries his hands and sits at the bench. He starts to assemble the 'floating hammer' optical illusion, as in Fig. 1.

DAVID: They've only gone and created antimatter *and* sustained it.

KATHY: Incredible.

DAVID: Thirty-eight atoms of antihydrogen for at least a tenth of a second.

KATHY: Wow, that's...that's not very long.

DAVID: Long enough to make detailed observations, and for the first time ever. Do you know what this means Kathy?

MRS. JONES: I know it's important to you David.

DAVID: Not just me Kathy, it could change the world...but if they find what we're really looking for, well, that could change the entire Universe.

MRS. JONES: I never really paid enough attention/

DAVID: Could you pass me that ruler?

MRS. JONES: What are you doing?

DAVID: Setting up a demo for my year eights.

MRS. JONES: OK.

She passes him the ruler and sits on a stool.

MRS. JONES: So what else have the Hydrogen Collidor people found out?

DAVID: Hadron Collidor.

MRS. JONES: I knew it was something like that.

DAVID: You don't want a science lesson Kathy.

MRS. JONES: Who wouldn't want to know news that could change the Universe...do you mean change in a bad way?

DAVID: I mean change the way we perceive the Universe *(Trails off.)* but then the Universe only exists because we perceive it.

MRS. JONES: David?

DAVID: Yes?...no, not in a bad way. No. Imagine accelerating to almost the speed of light around a seventeen mile circular tunnel before being smashed into another particle, creating new particles, new matter, stuff that could explain *everything*.

MRS. JONES: Wow...could you be more specific?

DAVID: Higgs boson.

MRS. JONES: Pardon?

DAVID: The Higgs boson.

MRS. JONES: Sounds American.

DAVID: Scottish.

MRS. JONES: Right, so who is he?

DAVID: It.

MRS. JONES: Sorry.

DAVID: Higgs is the name of the scientist that came up with the theory.

MRS. JONES: Theory?

DAVID: But not for long. Those boys at CERN/

MRS. JONES: The Hadron Collidor.

DAVID: Right. They're going to find it Kathy. And when they do, we will be able to observe the particle that gives things mass. We will be one step closer to understanding our most mysterious of forces. The force that binds the Universe.

He sets up his 'floating hammer' (Fig. 1) on the edge of a high shelf.

MRS. JONES: That is pretty remarkable.

DAVID: It's not magic.

MRS. JONES: It looks like it's going to fall.

DAVID: The trick is to find the centre of gravity.

MRS. JONES: And is that difficult?

DAVID: Adjust the length of the string, its position on the ruler, the angle of the hammer...like all good science it's trial and error.

MRS. JONES: Bit dangerous though. I mean if it does fall/

DAVID: It's not going to.

MRS. JONES: But if it does.

DAVID: I wouldn't let that happen.

MRS. JONES: You might not be able to stop it.

DAVID: Of course I could stop it!

MRS. JONES: Alright David, please, stay calm.

Pause.

DAVID: I dropped the girls off at their school first thing, then drove here. Routine. Except, I kept driving around the school, past the gate half a dozen times, deciding whether to come in today. I shouldn't have come in today. Why did I come in?

There must be a reason. There's always a reason. I need a reason. Kathy?

MRS. JONES: Otherwise you'd keep going round in circles?

DAVID: Right...exactly! So now I'm here I best make the most of it. Got a practical to prep for my year eights *(Looks at his watch.)* where does the time go?

DAVID disappears into a chemical store at the back, KATHY quickly gets up and checks the corridor before sitting back down. DAVID returns with a tray of bottled chemicals.

MRS. JONES: I thought you were doing this demonstration?

DAVID: As a starter, yes, then on to the main.

MRS. JONES: So what's gravity got to do with chemistry?

DAVID: It's all linked Kathy; forces, particles, atoms/

MRS. JONES: Antimatter, Higgs Boston.

DAVID: Boson.

MRS. JONES: They're year eight David, don't you think you'll just confuse them?

DAVID looks at the bottles, he becomes irritable.

DAVID: You see what I have to put up with.

MRS. JONES: What is it?

DAVID: I told them, I said if they mucked around there'd be no more praticals.

MRS. JONES: Has something gone missing?

He holds up one of the bottles.

DAVID: Do you think copper sulphate is meant to be that colour? Or have bits in the bottom? That precipitate is not meant to be in copper sulphate solution. Solution! That's the point. No solids, just solution. They're hopeless, they don't know how to measure out the right amounts, or weigh things accurately, record their results in an appropriate fashion and only half of them ever wear their safety goggles. They just mix it all together! Like they're six years old and making a mud pie in the kitchen, just chuck it all in and see what happens... no, no, no we can't have this can we.

He goes for the door, KATHY blocks his way.

MRS. JONES: Where are you going?

DAVID: I need to get to the chemical store, get some fresh samples.

MRS. JONES: I thought you said they weren't going to be doing the practical now?

DAVID: That doesn't mean we can't have fresh samples for other classes. I can't have *these* sitting on the shelf.

MRS. JONES: I'm afraid I can't let you leave David.

DAVID: What?

MRS. JONES: You're going to have to stay in here with me.

DAVID: Why?

Pause

MRS. JONES: Christ, do you have any idea how much trouble we're in?

DAVID: We?

MRS. JONES: Can you remember the last half an hour?

DAVID: Of course.

MRS. JONES: Everything?

DAVID: Yes, before you came in here I was next door with my year tens. We were extracting copper.

MRS. JONES: And how was the class?

DAVID: Disgusting, rude, same as usual.

MRS. JONES: Same as usual?

DAVID: Yes, that's the way they always are. That's why I'm constantly complaining about them. You know that.

MRS. JONES: So there wasn't any incident?

DAVID: Incident? Not that I...no.

MRS. JONES: Your sleeves David?

He slowly rolls them down, revealing that they are covered in spatters of blood. DAVID stands, confused, looking at himself.

DAVID: *(Muttering.)* That? I don't...potassium permanganate? Convection loop with year eight's yesterday... Iodine, preparing microscope slides with year seven's on Monday.

MRS. JONES: What about from today, this morning?

DAVID: Both industrial dyes, never come out, damn it.

MRS. JONES: What happened David?

DAVID: I don't know.

DAVID is unsteady, KATHY sits him on the stool. The bell goes for the end of break.

MRS. JONES: Let's just wait here, someone will be coming shortly.

DAVID: But my year eight class/

MRS. JONES: Don't worry, we've got it covered.

Pause. DAVID stares, then looks at his watch.

DAVID: Look at the time. Where does it go? If I could take it back. If I could just go back.

MRS. JONES: David? Can I get you anything?

Pause.

DAVID: Do you think I'm being punished because I don't believe in God?

SCENE 2

A cold, bright autumn day. The bottom of the playing field by the school fence. KYLE is kneeling down, cutting worms in half with a penknife. DAVID walks past, outside of the fence on the street. He wears a long wax coat and a wide brim hat. KYLE doesn't look at him.

KYLE: Thas the third time you've been past.

DAVID: Sorry?

KYLE: Y'walkin' round the school?

DAVID: It's almost a perfect circle, isn't it.

KYLE: Reminds me of a boxin' ring.

DAVID: Isn't that more of a square?

KYLE: Not the shape.

   Pause.

DAVID: Do they allow knives in school now?

KYLE: It's for an experiment.

DAVID: And what have those poor worms done to you?

KYLE: Y'get two.

DAVID: Pardon?

KYLE: Y'get two, if y'cut one in 'alf.

DAVID: That's a myth I'm afraid.

KYLE: I'm doin' 'em a favour, y'get two.

DAVID: The brain is at one end, the guts are the other. We need both to live, so do they. I'm afraid all you get when you cut a worm in half is two bits of dead worm.

KYLE: That right?

DAVID: Nothing's right Kyle, just an educated guess.

KYLE recognises him.

KYLE: Mr. Milford? Haven't seen y'f'time Sir.

DAVID: *(Amused.)* For *time*? Any specific length?

KYLE: Where's y'beard?

DAVID: I shaved it off. Fifteen years I had that thing.

KYLE: Now tha's time.

DAVID: Needed a change.

KYLE: And you've gone thin...why didn't y'come back this year Sir?

DAVID: I haven't been very well Kyle.

KYLE: Y'look OK to me.

DAVID: You said I looked thin.

KYLE: Yeah but y'looked fat before.

DAVID: I'm guessing that's a compliment.

KYLE: Y'do a lot of guessing don't you Sir.

DAVID: How have lessons been?

KYLE: Oh, y'know, supply teachers. Loads of
worksheets, no practicals, no control. Just tryin'
t'get to the end of the lesson and out the door
quick as possible. Worksheets though Sir, slow
seconds down to minutes, know what I mean?

DAVID: *(Distant.)* Like approaching the speed of light.

KYLE: Not goin' anywhere. You OK Mr. Milford?

DAVID: The school looks so small from here.

KYLE: Furthest possible point. I worked it out.

DAVID: What are you doing down here Kyle?

KYLE: Only place I can find worms Sir.

DAVID: What about your mates?

KYLE: I'd get in trouble f'cuttin' them in 'alf.

DAVID: No I mean why aren't you hanging out with
your/

KYLE: What you doin' walkin' round the school?

DAVID: Tracing a path.

KYLE: Like the planets orbitin' the sun?

DAVID: Not quite.

KYLE: I remember y'sayin' the light from the sun
takes eight minutes to reach us.

DAVID: Approximately.

KYLE: So the sun could 'ave blown up and we wouldn't know for another eight minutes.

DAVID: Well our sun doesn't have the critical mass to...actually, it's hard to say what would happen if our star went supernova.

KYLE: Y'don't seem very sure of anythin' Sir.

DAVID: Heisenberg's Uncertainty Principle. Nothing is definite. There is no single, definite result for an observation, only a number of different *possible* outcomes and their *probabilities.*

KYLE: Eh?

DAVID: Ever heard of Schrödinger's cat?

KYLE: I've got a cat.

DAVID: Look it up Kyle, Schrödinger's cat.

KYLE takes out a pen and scribbles on his hand. He looks at the sun.

KYLE: I read on the internet the world's gonna end anyway Sir. They're buildin' this Big Bang machine, gonna make a black hole, the Halo Collapser or somethin'?

DAVID: The Large Hadron Collidor.

KYLE: Thas it, gonna make a black hole right 'ere on Earth, suck us all up.

DAVID: Not quite Kyle. In fact it's likely going to help us find more substance in the universe, new particles, antimatter.

KYLE: Antimatter?

DAVID: 'Stuff' that travels backwards through time. They might even discover evidence of extra dimensions.

KYLE: What like the Marvel Multiverse? Thas only in comic books.

DAVID: How many dimensions do we live in?

KYLE: It's three innit?

DAVID: Four if you include time, but some theories suggest that there might be eleven dimensions.

KYLE: Where?

DAVID: They exist, just that they're so thin we can't see them. You believe atoms exist don't you, but you can't see them.

KYLE: Yeah but, *eleven* dimensions? Sounds like bollocks...Sir.

DAVID: Maybe it is a bit difficult to understand.

KYLE: Suppose y'want me to look that up as well.

KYLE moves back to his worms.

DAVID: Imagine one of your earthworms, but *completely* flat. A two-dimensional creature, living on a sheet of paper. How many directions can it travel in?

KYLE: Forwards, backwards...?

DAVID: And?

KYLE: Side to side...up and down?

DAVID: Two-dimensional remember, not even the thickness of the paper, so *no* up and down. Just forward, backward, left and right. Then one day along comes Kyle, the three-dimensional creature and says 'hey, there is an up and down as well you know.' What do you think our 2D creature, who wouldn't even be able to *perceive* anything three-dimensional, what do you think they would say back to you?

KYLE: Probably tell me I was talking bollocks...Sir.

DAVID: Exactly, they wouldn't believe you, just like we find it hard to believe that there are more dimensions out there that we can't perceive. That doesn't mean they're not there, doesn't mean it's not possible, or indeed probable.

Pause.

KYLE: Y'said somethin' about time travel Sir.

DAVID: Time travel?

KYLE: Whas antimatter?

DAVID: Stuff which is the opposite of matter in every way. It has a negative mass, opposite charge, and just like all *matter* in the universe travels forwards through time, *antimatter* travels backwards through time.

KYLE: And they're gonna make this stuff? Thas crazy.

DAVID: Problem is when it meets matter, both are instantly annihilated. And as we're surrounded by matter, it doesn't last long enough to be observed, until now.

KYLE: The Collidor.

DAVID: Exactly, when they fire that machine up for the first time/

KYLE: Seen a picture of it Sir. This massive circular tunnel, deep underground, said it's made of magnets or somethin'.

DAVID: And those magnets help accelerate particles to almost the speed of light around these tunnels before smashing them into other particles, creating quarks, antimatter, but *most* importantly/

KYLE: That what y'doin' walkin' round the school Sir?

DAVID: Pardon?

KYLE: Y'said somethin' about approachin' the speed of light, y'said you was tracin' a path.

Pause.

DAVID: Just helps me think Kyle.

KYLE: Never know who y'gonna bump into though, eh Sir.

Pause.

KYLE: When y'comin' back to Science Mr. Milford? I mean I know we ain't gonna be able to make antimatter or anythin' but/

DAVID: You're a good lad Kyle.

KYLE: Thanks Sir, but I weren't asking for that.

Pause.

DAVID: I can't be sure.

KYLE: So you ain't comin' back?

DAVID: I didn't say that/

KYLE: Is this that Uncertainty bollocks again...alright, what are the *possibilities* of y'comin' back?

A football rolls on in KYLE's direction.

REECE: *(Off.)* Ball!...Ball!

KYLE distracts himself with the worms. DAVID puts his hat back on. REECE approaches KYLE, CHANTAY behind him filming on her phone.

REECE: Ball... Ball!... Ball!! Y'deaf or somethin'?!

CHANTAY: Leave 'im alone Reece, he's talkin' to his dad. That is y'dad ain't it Kyle?

KYLE: No.

REECE: Ain't y'mum ever told y'bout talkin'
t'strangers? He could be a pederast or anythin'.
Looks like a pederast.

CHANTAY: Don't worry, I've got 'im. Pervert.

DAVID: I'm going to get on my way Kyle.

KYLE ignores him. DAVID looks at the other two before walking off. CHANTAY films.

CHANTAY: Thas it, on y'way perv. 'Member I'm
watchin' you!

REECE: It ain't 'is fault Chantay, Kyle 'ere is such a
pretty boy who could resist?

KYLE: Piss off.

REECE: Big boy usin' cus words now? Why don't
y'come and play football, show us you ain't just all
chat?

CHANTAY: Leave 'im Reece, 'e don't look that
bothered.

REECE: We're one man down!

CHANTAY: 'Cos you crippled 'im!

CHANTAY turns the camera back up the field.

REECE: Come on Kyle, we need t'make up the
numbers.

REECE starts bouncing the ball off KYLE's head.

REECE: Come on, enough of y'bollocks. Y'might enjoy it.

KYLE: Piss off Reece.

REECE: I'll let you 'ave that one, and the last one, if you come and play...'ere Chantay, you checkin' this.

CHANTAY: *(To camera.)* You used to come down 'ere for a crafty fag at break, we do the same.

REECE: Chantay, you gettin' this?

CHANTAY: Shut it will ya.

REECE stops, he puts the ball in front of KYLE lining himself up to kick it point blank into his face.

REECE: This is gonna be good Chantay, you've gorra get this.

CHANTAY: *(To camera.)* Teachers say 'ello, ones who liked you anyways.

REECE: This is gonna be a belter, Chantay!

CHANTAY: It ain't all about you Reece!

KYLE grabs the ball when REECE is distracted and stabs it with his penknife.

REECE: You stupid prick!

REECE steps up to him. KYLE stands, still wielding the pen knife. CHANTAY turns the camera on them.

REECE: Wha?... What?!

KYLE: What d'you reckon?

REECE: You owe me a ball, and then some. Freak.

REECE backs away and exits. CHANTAY films KYLE as he cautiously puts away the knife.

CHANTAY: Teachers'd go mental if they knew you 'ad that.

KYLE: Y'gonna tell?

CHANTAY: Nah, but I could show 'em.

KYLE: Y'gonna?

CHANTAY: Would you 'ave done 'im?

KYLE: Probably.

CHANTAY: Blokes. Always 'as to end the same doesn't it.

KYLE: Not always. Anythin's possible.

KYLE flattens the ball and holds it up.

KYLE: If you was a two-dimensional creature, would y'believe there was a three-dimensional world out there?

CHANTAY: Eh?

KYLE: Nothin'.

CHANTAY: *(To camera.)* This is Kyle, 'e's a bit like you. Not quite 'ere...say 'ello to my brother Kyle.

KYLE: 'Lo.

CHANTAY: How about another thought for the day, I like 'em.

KYLE: If you could travel back in time, what would y'change?

SCENE 3

Early January. MRS. JONES' office. Files and papers everywhere, which she is trying to organise. DAVID enters, he's holding a file.

DAVID: Knock knock?

MRS. JONES: David, how lovely to see you.

He puts his hand out, she gives him a hug.

DAVID: I brought the S.E.N. data you wanted.

MRS. JONES: Data?

DAVID: For the year tens.

MRS. JONES: Ah, key stage four...that side of the room.

DAVID: Having a clear out?

MRS. JONES: Orders from the Headmaster, slave-driving shit.

DAVID: Can I help?

MRS. JONES: This data's help enough David, that's exactly what I'm missing. And you just know that's the set they're going to want to look at.

DAVID: They?

MRS. JONES: Rumours of an inspection.

DAVID: Always rumours of an inspection.

MRS. JONES: I have a horrible feeling this time they might be true...too many gaps. And they want everything to be tight. Tight, tight, tight like a duck's arse!... So uptight.

DAVID: It's not nice being observed.

MRS. JONES: Do you not think I do a fair job?

DAVID: I meant when the shoe is on the other foot Kathy.

MRS. JONES: I know what you *mean* David, and I know what you're thinking. I know what all the teaching staff think, but just because I'm not a teacher, doesn't mean I can't recognise the *quality* in teaching standards.

DAVID: I just meant that we'd all be under the same pressure/

MRS. JONES: Pressure? You don't need to talk to me about pressure. Looking after the welfare of these kids is a full-time job. The parents can't do it, so it's down to me. And what *teachers* don't understand is that a pastoral role can be physically and emotionally draining, so then to have to chase up and file all their data as well! I keep telling the Head, we need another member of staff because it's driving me around the bloody bend!...sorry David.

Pause. KATHY looks around.

MRS. JONES: Still, a clear out will do me good. You know what they say. Tidy desk, tidy mind... So, how's yours?

DAVID: My desk?

MRS. JONES: No...well, yes.

DAVID: Immaculate.

MRS. JONES: And your *(Taps her head.)* you know.

DAVID: Oh, that's...yes, much better.

MRS. JONES: So not immaculate then.

DAVID: Well I wouldn't say/

MRS. JONES: But scrubbing up well?

DAVID: Getting there.

MRS. JONES: Please.

KATHY offers her seat and then perches on the desk in front of him.

MRS. JONES: It's a terrible affliction. I'm not unfamiliar with feeling a bit fed up, you know? I remember during my college days, drinking like a fish/

DAVID: I don't drink.

MRS. JONES: Right. Neither do I, not anymore. Not excessively anyway. But oh God was I miserable back then. Black clothes, gothic music, and I don't mind telling you I used to self-harm *(She does the action, almost comically.)* you know? The physical pain to take away the mental anguish, and all that...anyway, I've left it all well behind me. I just woke up one day and threw it all out, my CDs, my clothes. Deciding life was for living, you know?

Pause.

DAVID: I couldn't find all of the data for year tens. I'm assuming the supply teacher didn't record it on the system, so I'll have to trawl through some of their coursework to fill in the blanks.

MRS. JONES: The sooner the better, of course, but I do want to make sure that you're settled first. It's not just the pupils' welfare I'm interested in...how's your wife?

DAVID: She's...she's a rock.

MRS. JONES: She's suffered as well hasn't she? God, I hope it's not contagious!...and your hobby, stargazing or something?

DAVID: Cosmology, yes.

MRS. JONES: And you've got one of those funny domes in the back of your garden, haven't you?

DAVID: An observatory, well, a very small one.

MRS. JONES: So what's going on in the big wide universe then?

DAVID: Oh it's ever-changing. I have a beautiful view of Europa at the moment as it passes in front of Jupiter.

MRS. JONES: That is amazing! What is it, a spaceship?

DAVID: It's one of Jupiter's moons.

MRS. JONES: Wow, a moon! We've got one of those.

DAVID: Not like this one. A great, scarred ball of ice. Orbiting our most majestic gas giant. And of course where there's water, there's the possibility, just the slightest possibility of/

MRS. JONES: Flooding?

DAVID: Life.

MRS. JONES: Aliens?!

DAVID: Well, not like you think. If anything, microscopic bacteria in rivers miles beneath the frozen surface. And to be honest, probably not. But still, a possibility.

MRS. JONES: That is amazing.

DAVID: I also discovered a star.

MRS. JONES: Doesn't that mean you get to name it?

DAVID: Well, letters and numbers, yes.

MRS. JONES: That's a bit disappointing.

DAVID: I used my wife's initials and her birth date.

MRS. JONES: That is so lovely David...but it does sound a bit obsessive?

DAVID: It is. Completely engrossing.

MRS. JONES: Remember what I said about my college days David, about losing those old habits.

DAVID: I'm hardly pickling my liver.

MRS. JONES: Quite, maybe it's just me. It always made me feel small and insignificant looking up into the night sky. And who would want to occupy themselves with something that makes them feel small and insignificant? *(She takes his hand.)* We want you back down here, both feet firmly on the ground.

There's a knock on the door before REECE and CHANTAY, preoccupied with her mobile, enter. MRS. JONES lets go of DAVID's hand

MRS. JONES: Ah Reece, just the boy.

REECE: Miss...y'alright Sir, y'comin' back to Science?

MRS. JONES: Mr. Milford will be back teaching as of next week, but you will see him around school for the rest of this week.

REECE: Where've y'been sir?

MRS. JONES: He's been on holiday Reece, now leave the man alone.

REECE: 'As he lost his voice Miss? Thas one big ass holiday Sir.

DAVID: I've been looking after my wife if you must know Reece, she's not been very well.

MRS. JONES: That's right Reece, he's not been very well/

DAVID: My wife/

MRS. JONES: His *wife's* not been very well.

REECE: So why d'y'lie then Miss?

MRS. JONES: Because it's none of your business!

REECE: Just askin'.

DAVID: How's science been Reece?

MRS. JONES: Reece has been smashing test tubes against the wall in science this morning, that's why we have the pleasure of his company.

REECE: It's this supply teacher Sir, he's a complete f... idiot.

DAVID: I'm sure he thinks the world of you.

REECE: Eh, what's not to like? Nah Sir, anyway, when y'comin' back? Cos I swear we have him one more time I'm gonna lamp him.

MRS. JONES: Reece.

REECE: What Miss, I'm sayin' Sir's good. I enjoy Science when Sir's there. I learn stuff and stuff.

Ain't that right Chantay, that supply teacher's shit in't he.

MRS. JONES: Reece!

REECE: Nah, but y'know, I'm biggin' up Sir. Ain't that right Chantay?

CHANTAY: Dunno, don't remember 'im.

MRS. JONES: Chantay, how can you say that? It's Mr. Milford.

REECE: *(Jeers.)* Milford!

DAVID: Well, I have lost the beard.

MRS. JONES: And the belly, I forgot to mention how dashing you looked.

REECE: You're in there Sir.

DAVID: And I did only teach Chantay for a couple of months before I went away.

REECE: He's been inside! What d'y'do Sir? Rob a bank? Shank someone?

DAVID: You really don't remember me?

CHANTAY shrugs.

MRS. JONES: Chantay's been going through a rough time at the moment.

CHANTAY: Thanks Miss!

MRS. JONES: Don't worry Chantay, we're all friends here.

CHANTAY: *(Mumbles.)* I ain't y'friend.

MRS. JONES: So, Reece, what are we going to do with you? You're already on report, you've got enough backed up detentions to last you a lifetime...and will you please tuck your shirts in and do up your ties both of you! Come on, top button and all.

REECE: Sir ain't got 'is top button done!

MRS. JONES: Well I'm sure he won't mind leading by example... David?

REECE: Yeah *David.*

DAVID looks at KATHY, then starts to do his top button. The other two comply, REECE is grinning at him.

KATHY: Good, we never know who's going to be checking up, do we.

The phone rings. KATHY picks it up.

MRS. JONES: Hello...yes he's here with me now... lovely, we'll pop down *(She hangs up.)* Speak of the devil, the Headmaster would like to see you David. Probably just to give you the once over, make sure you're not foaming at the mouth. And I'm going to have to see the Head about this latest incident Reece. We just can't be going on like this. You two wait for me here please, and hands to yourself!

DAVID and MRS. JONES go to leave, an out of breath KYLE bumps into them at the door. He carries a closed shoebox, he thrusts into DAVID's hands while he recovers.

KYLE: Sir...I 'eard you were back...I wanted to...show you somethin'...

KATHY takes it from DAVID's hands and gives it back to KYLE.

MRS. JONES: But not just now Kyle.

DAVID: Get your breath back Kyle, I'll be back in a moment. Then tell me all / about it.

MRS. JONES: Now please Mr. Milford.

DAVID follows KATHY out.

REECE: *(Shouts.)* Come back to science Sir!

REECE pushes a pile of folders off a chair and sits

REECE: *(To KYLE.)* Gay boy.

CHANTAY: I ain't hangin' round 'ere Reece.

REECE: Come on, we've got a chance to wind up Milly Milford. Good old Mildred, *David*...'ere, d'y'reckon 'im and Miss are doin' it?

CHANTAY: I'm goin' down the shop, gettin' some chips. You want anythin'?

REECE: Fags.

CHANTAY: Y'don't need nothin', eh Kyle, looks like you've already got y'packed lunch...or is that another one of your freaky experiments?

She tries to take a look, KYLE pulls it away from her.

REECE: What you chattin' to 'im for?!

CHANTAY: *(Shrugs.)* ...laters.

She fiddles with her phone as she exits.

REECE: So what's in the box gay boy?

KYLE: Y'can't open it.

REECE: Oh I'm sorry, is it a secret? Some kinda magic trick?

KYLE: No.

REECE: Let's 'ave a look then.

KYLE: It's based on Schrödinger's cat, 'cept this is a frog.

REECE: Wha'you on about?

KYLE: Wha'd'you care?

REECE: I wouldn't ask otherwise, would I y'mong.

KYLE: Well first you 'ave to imagine a piece of radioactive material that when decays triggers a device which releases a deadly poison.

REECE: Yeah, I know radioactive shit is dangerous.

KYLE: Somethin' like that. Schrödinger reckons that if y'put a cat in box f'one hour with a small amount of this radioactive material, that *may* or *may not* decay in that hour, it's impossible to tell whether the cat's dead or alive. 'Cept this is a frog, and I haven't got any radioactive material.

REECE: Why don't y'just look?

KYLE: Y'can't look. The act of lookin' means y'can tell whether the cat's dead or alive.

REECE: So if you don't look, you can't tell whether the cat's dead or alive?...big tits!

KYLE: I don't quite get it myself, thas why I was gonna ask Sir.

REECE: Y'such an arse licker.

KYLE: I think what it means is if you don't look, you can say that the cat is both dead, and alive, at the same time.

REECE: *(Flustered.)* What a load of bollocks!

He grabs the box, throws it on the floor and stamps on it repeatedly.

REECE: S'dead now, no need to look.

KYLE picks up the battered box and stares at it.

REECE: See I knew Science was fun...I ain't hangin' round here, got fags t'smoke. Laters gay frog boy.

He goes. KYLE sits, looking at the box. DAVID and MRS. JONES enter.

MRS. JONES: You see that's the problem with our dear Headmaster, there's always something that takes priority over our affairs.

DAVID: He did seem quite stressed.

MRS. JONES: Well aren't we all David, aren't we all... Kyle, where's Reece gone?

KYLE storms out of the room, leaving the battered box.

DAVID: Kyle? Kyle?!

MRS. JONES: Let him go.

DAVID: No I...he had something to show me. *(He looks at the battered box.)* Looks like Reece got there first.

MRS. JONES: Well there's no point in giving him another detention, you'll just be adding to the pile.

DAVID: So how are we meant to discipline him?

MRS. JONES: You leave that to me and the Head. We're looking to use the extra funding we get, for accommodating pupils like Reece, to implement a system they've been trying in some inner-city schools across/

DAVID: Are we going back to Assertive Discipline?

MRS. JONES: God no, nothing like that. This system, well, it seems pretty radical on the surface, but the results have been really quite positive.

DAVID: So what are we meant to do with Reece in the mean time?

MRS. JONES: Deal with him as best you can.

DAVID: He needs to be brought down a peg or two.

MRS. JONES: Remember we're always here to take him off your hands if he gets too much.

DAVID: I'd better go and see if Kyle's OK...oh, that data, I/

MRS. JONES: Just leave it on the table David. I'll sort it when I can.

He puts the file down on her desk, and goes to leave.

MRS. JONES: And David!

DAVID: Yes?

MRS. JONES: It's good to have you back.

DAVID: Yes.

He's gone. MRS. JONES looks through the file he has left.

MRS. JONES: Immaculate.

She spots the battered box, picks it up and opens it. She grimaces, closes it, and throws it in the bin.

SCENE 4

A science lab, it is immaculate. Only the top end of the lab is represented: the teacher's bench and the front set of pupil benches. There are gas taps and a sink/tap on the benches. There is a door leading off to a small storeroom.

On the pupil benches; card, sellotape, Blu-tack and two different sized lenses for each pupil. On the teacher's bench, apparatus to test the Absorption of Radiation; a Geiger-Müler counter, a box of radioactive samples and barriers of aluminium foil. The

Geiger counter clicks intermittently as it picks up background radiation.

Late February, lunchtime. KYLE is carefully putting samples into the reading equipment; he is using forceps and wearing protective clothing, gloves and goggles. DAVID observes, he has just finished his lunch and is sipping a mug of coffee.

KYLE: Not meant to eat in the lab Sir.

DAVID: Have you had your lunch Kyle?

KYLE: Not hungry.

DAVID: You need to eat Kyle, otherwise you can't function properly.

KYLE: Me goggles are steamin' up.

DAVID: You can take those off, but gloves and forceps are essential, this can be pretty unpleasant stuff.

KYLE puts the sample in place, facing the counter. The count goes up.

DAVID: Make a note of the reading.

KYLE: *(Writing.)* Sounds broke.

DAVID: It's picking up radiation from the source, in this case a sample of Strontium-90.

KYLE: Which is Beta radiation, right?

DAVID: Firing out tiny electrons.

KYLE: So this is the stuff Schrödinger used in 'is experiment.

DAVID: Well he didn't actually do the experiment. It was a thought experiment, a theoretical experiment.

KYLE: Where's the fun in that?

DAVID: Now place the aluminium shield in front of the source.

KYLE does so. The count falls.

DAVID: Don't forget to make a note *(KYLE does so.)* So, Beta radiation can be stopped by thin sheets of aluminium.

KYLE: Not very powerful.

DAVID: It doesn't quite work like that.

KYLE continues with the experiment, picking up another sample, taking readings, making notes etc.

DAVID: Now that is Alpha radiation, two protons, two neutrons, so it's much bigger and heavier than Beta. It doesn't travel very far and is easily stopped by a sheet of paper, so doesn't seem very powerful, but at short range it's the most damaging. It can damage cells in the skin externally, but if you swallow it then you're in all kinds of trouble. In fact, all of these sources of radiation can be lethal in the right/

KYLE: *(Picks up a sample.)* Whas this? Why's it in concrete?

DAVID: This is Gamma, the most penetrative radiation, which is why we have to keep it in a thick shield.

KYLE: Gamma? I know that made 'Hulk Mad!'

DAVID: Gamma radiation penetrates the furthest because there is no particle. It's a wave and not a particle, like the neutron, proton and electron...but you see, this is where we get into new territory.

KYLE: No Hulk though?

DAVID: No. I'm afraid if you expose someone to a high dose of Gamma radiation they're more likely to get cancer than become superhuman.

Pause.

KYLE: Don't they use Gamma to treat cancer?

DAVID: Sounds strange, but yes they use high doses of Gamma radiation to destroy cancer cells. It's very clever really, you see they set up/

KYLE: I know Sir, they fire loads of beams of low radiation into the body at different angles, makin' the beams cross over where the cancer is. So the low radiation doesn't damage the body where it passes through, but gets really high at the place they cross over, killin' the cancer.

DAVID: Very good Kyle. Of course none of this would have been possible without Marie Curie, who discovered radiation but unfortunately died of cancer from exposure.

KYLE: Silly cow.

DAVID: She wasn't to know was she, and look what good has come from it.

KYLE: Dad died of cancer Sir.

DAVID: I know that Kyle.

KYLE: No y'don't.

Pause. KYLE continues with the experiment.

KYLE: I don't get how the cat can be both dead and alive.

DAVID: Until we observe it, we can't say that it's either. So we have to say it's both. It's like light, or the electron. Light travels in waves, we talk about light *flooding* a room, but it's made up of tiny particles called photons. The electron in Schrödinger's experiment. When it's observed, it behaves like a particle, existing in a fixed point in space. However, when it's not being observed, it behaves like a wave. It exists everywhere all at once.

KYLE: So...are we 'ere?

DAVID: Of course we are. I can see you, you can see me...but that doesn't mean we can't be somewhere else as well. We *could* be in lots of different places at the same time.

KYLE: So my dad, he could be somewhere else?

DAVID: *(Pause.)* It's at this point I'm meant to backtrack Kyle, tell you it's not like that, but... anything's possible.

KYLE cuts a star shape from a piece of paper, he holds it up

KYLE: See 'ow I made a star, but I also made the shape of a star in the paper? Somethin' identical to the star, but not made of anythin' we can see. And it doesn't matter wha' shape I cut out *(Cuts a circle.)* I always get this 'negative' twin.

DAVID: The theory of antimatter. Someone's been doing their research.

KYLE: Still see 'is outline at the breakfast table. 'E left a big 'ole but I know 'e's still there *(Pause.)* So this antimatter, *definitely* travels backwards through time?

DAVID: In theory, yes. Positrons, antiprotons, antineutrons all travel back/

KYLE: But they're tiny aren't they?

DAVID: They've also managed to make antihydrogen, unfortunately not for long enough to observe yet, but when they fire up the/

KYLE: Yeah but antihydrogen, couldn't make a ship out of it could you. So whas the point?

DAVID: A ship?

KYLE: *(Frustrated.)* A time machine.

DAVID: You have to start small Kyle. You're doing well enough to understand Einstein, Heisenberg, Dirac and even Schrödinger. Stick with that for the time being.

The bell goes for the end of lunch.

DAVID: Now you've missed a lot of time this year, but if we can just get you through this assessment, we can move you back up into a set where you belong. Then you'll be in a much better position to ask these big questions. Yes?

DAVID heads off stage to the door at the back of the class. KYLE continues to take readings.

DAVID: *(Off.)* Right you lot! If you think you're coming into my lab behaving like that...Jordan, stop chewing! Katie, tie on, now! Right, in an orderly fashion... Orderly!

DAVID comes back in as kids pour into the classroom. CHANTAY comes in and sits on the front desk, she is playing with her phone.

DAVID: Reece, down at the front please...Reece!

REECE: *(Off.)* He's got my pen!

DAVID: I don't care Reece, get yourself down here now!

REECE comes in and sits next to CHANTAY, he's still mouthing off at someone at the back of the class. A paper ball flies on in his direction.

DAVID: I saw that Jordan, so you can stay behind after class and clean this entire floor. Got it?!... Now I did promise you that we'd do something fun today/

CHANTAY: *(Dry.)* Yeah, fun.

DAVID: However...Chantay, could you put that away please...however, if this is going to be your attitude, then we'll sit and do worksheets for the rest of the lesson. Your choice.

The class settle.

DAVID: Better. OK. Now in front of you, you'll find some equipment...yes Alisha... Oh, sorry, one minute.

DAVID picks up a set of pupil equipment and takes it to the back of the class. REECE gets up and approaches the Geiger counter as DAVID re-enters.

REECE: Whas all this Sir?

DAVID: It's a Geiger counter, used to measure radiation. Now could you please sit down.

REECE grabs the box of samples, reading.

REECE: Radioactive? Sick!

DAVID: Don't touch that Reece! It's not for you. In fact it's time these went away. Kyle, could you join the rest of the class please.

DAVID takes the samples back off REECE and packs them away. KYLE and REECE sit at the front, either side of CHANTAY.

REECE: 'Ow come Kyle gets t'do the sick experiments Sir?

DAVID: Well are you prepared to give up your lunchtimes to further your knowledge?

REECE: Nah.

DAVID: So.

CHANTAY: But Sir, it looks interestin'.

DAVID: Actually Chantay, I want you to make your own devices to measure radiation, with the materials I've supplied. *(He addresses the class.)* So, any ideas?

CHANTAY: Bits of paper and glass?

REECE: Look like Mr. Murphy's glasses. *(He holds them up to his eyes, mocking.)* 'What is History? History is evidence, evidence, evidence...'

DAVID: Put them down Reece. Now come on, what instrument do we use to look at things?

CHANTAY: Er, telly?

DAVID: No, we watch the television. We don't use it to look at things.

REECE: Yeah, I use it to *look at* Match of the Day.

DAVID: Does anyone have a sensible suggestion?

Pause.

KYLE: Is it a telescope Sir?

DAVID: Spot on Kyle.

REECE: *(Slurp.)*

CHANTAY: I thought we were gonna make somethin' to do with radiation?

DAVID: Well what do you think telescopes pick up?

CHANTAY: Pick up? Like with their 'ands?

DAVID: No, what do we use telescopes for?

REECE: To look at stars and shit.

DAVID: Reece.

REECE: Stuff Sir, I said stuff.

DAVID: So what do stars give out so that we can see them?

CHANTAY: Give out? I don't get it Sir, like givin' out flyers or sweets?... Stars? What?!

KYLE: Light, Sir.

REECE: *(Two successive slurps.)*

DAVID: That's right, stars give out light, that's how we detect them.

CHANTAY: But Sir, radiation?

KYLE: Light is a kind of radiation.

REECE: Bollo... Rubbish! Radiation's like mutant stuff, melts y'face off and everythin'.

DAVID: And what happens if you stay in the sun too long Reece?

CHANTAY: Oh I get it, sunburn. Never thought about it like that.

REECE: Easy Chantay *(Gestures to KYLE.)* y'startin' t'sound like gimp-boy 'ere.

DAVID: Has everyone got the idea? You're going to try and build your own telescope. Have a little think about the design, then off you go.

The pupils start the task.

CHANTAY: What got you into Science Sir?

DAVID: Me? The mystery of the force that binds us, the hunt for the nature of gravity. And we might just be there. It's not only antimatter they'll be able to make in the Large Hadron Collider, but hopefully, and for the first time, the most elusive particle in science. The Higgs boson.

REECE: So it wasn't cos you liked to blow things up then?

DAVID: That as well. *(Laughs.)* I remember one of my friends at Uni. Dan. Complete nutter. He was breaking the sticks off firework rockets, lighting them, then chucking them down the toilet. They'd whizz around on the surface of the water before going off. That is until one disappeared around the U-bend. Of course when it went off in that confined space, it blew the back out of the toilet, flooding the place.

KYLE: Sick.

DAVID: The funny thing was, in order to avoid a fine from the landlord, he went out, bought a toilet, and refitted it within twenty-four hours. I just remember thinking how *resourceful* that was...and I'll never forget sitting on a bus with him, driving through Leeds, while he's cradling a brand new, ceramic toilet in his arms.

CHANTAY: That's a well funny story Sir.

REECE: Yeah, that's nothin'. I shoved a rocket up my next door neighbours cat's arse. Stick'n'all. Now when that went off in a confined space, it must 'ave made a right mess of its insides. Took a while for it t'die though, could 'ear it cryin' in pain all night.

CHANTAY: *(Hits him.)* You're a bastard Reece.

REECE: What's that for, only a stupid cat.

DAVID addresses the class.

DAVID: Right, how are we doing?... Lovely work Alisha, looking good...stop wasting the sellotape please Kirsten!... Right *(Gestures to a window.)* now we're lucky enough to have a daylight moon this afternoon, so we might get the chance to observe some of its features.

REECE: I ain't gonna use mine to look at the moon Sir, I'm gonna check out what's goin' on in those bedroom windows across the road.

DAVID: You won't be looking at anything at this rate. Before even attempting to attach the lenses, try and get the basic cone structure first Reece.

REECE: Like a big spliff yeah Sir? Bong!

DAVID: Now the moon doesn't make its own light, so where does the light come from?

REECE: Kyle's arse Sir.

CHANTAY: Ain't it reflecting the light from the sun?

DAVID: Excellent Chantay.

CHANTAY: Standard Sir.

REECE: *(Frustrated.)* I can't do this!

DAVID: 'Course you can Reece.

REECE: I'd like to see you try Sir.

DAVID: Actually I've got one I prepared earlier.

DAVID goes into the storeroom. REECE immediately jumps up and starts turning on the water taps in the sink, nothing comes out.

KYLE: What y'doin'?

REECE: Tryin' t'flood this dump. Where's the water?

CHANTAY finishes her telescope and holds it up to her eye looking at KYLE.

CHANTAY: I see you.

KYLE: Y'like watchin', don't you.

CHANTAY: Dunno what y'gonna miss.

KYLE: How come you film everythin'?

CHANTAY: Makin' a documentary.

KYLE: For telly?

CHANTAY: Nah, for my brother. He's in the army, posted in the Middle East. I like to keep 'im in check.

REECE: Wha', like he's missin' somethin' 'ere?!

CHANTAY: It makes me feel like 'e's with me, alright!

KYLE: It's the same with my cat.

CHANTAY: What, y'film stuff for y'cat?

KYLE: Nah, he reminds me of...dunt matter.

REECE: I ever get 'old of your cat Kyle, I'm gonna shove a rocket up its arse.

REECE is holding a lit lighter by one of the gas taps, he stops when DAVID comes back in holding a real telescope.

DAVID: Water and gas have been turned off at the mains Reece, do you take me for a complete idiot?

REECE: What Sir, I weren't doin' nothin'.

DAVID: You want to busy your hands Reece, why don't you come over here and look at this.

CHANTAY uses her telescope to try and get a fix on the moon. DAVID's comes with a little stand, which he sets up on a bench close by, getting it in focus.

REECE: You didn't make that telescope Sir, y'bought it!

DAVID: Alright, so I cheated a bit, but theirs should work just as well.

REECE: Work it Kyle, come on, work it. Sir's askin' y'to work it boy.

DAVID: OK class, you don't have a stand so the trick is to have a steady hand. Think about it like aiming a gun, you've got to try and keep the target in your sights.

CHANTAY: Don't want to do this no more Sir.

DAVID: You need to get right up to the eyepiece.

REECE: Ring piece!

DAVID: Erm, Jordan, seeing as you haven't finished, why don't you come and take a look through this telescope?

REECE: Thought y'said I could 'ave a go!

DAVID: All in good time Reece. Jordan! Put Amy down and/

REECE: Give it 'ere.

REECE grabs the telescope from DAVID and looks through it. Pause.

REECE: Eh I've got it Sir, I've got it! I can see the moon and all the craters and shit! Thas pretty cool...so is there like a dark side to the moon Sir?

REECE has pulled away from the telescope. He has a black ring of boot polish around his eye. The class start to laugh.

REECE: Wha'? Ah forget I asked. I ain't no science geek.

DAVID: No Reece, it's an interesting question. The moon is gravitationally locked by the Earth, which means there is a side that always faces the Earth. So there's a side we don't see. But it's not dark, it gets cycles of day and night just like earth.

CHANTAY: I like it when it's completely dark Sir.

DAVID: That's called a New Moon.

CHANTAY: Totally black Sir. Like a *big black circle*...in the sky like.

DAVID: Quite, well, I'd better go and put this away. Might not look like much but it's a useful piece of kit, I'm sure you'll agree.

DAVID goes.

REECE: Whas the deal with you?

CHANTAY: *(Smirking.)* Nothin'.

REECE: Come on, spit it out.

CHANTAY: Check y'face.

CHANTAY hands REECE a make-up mirror. He looks at himself, wipes off the black. He loses his temper. He goes for KYLE.

CHANTAY: Reece, it was nothin' t'do with 'im!

REECE tries to smash a stool but fails. The class have fallen quiet. REECE looks around, then takes the radioactive samples and drops them in DAVID's coffee.

KYLE: Reece, what y'playin' at?

REECE: Taste of his own medicine.

KYLE: Don't mess about with that, thas proper dangerous.

REECE: You'd know wouldn't ya.

KYLE: Serious Reece, that ain't a joke.

REECE finishes, grabs KYLE by the neck and holds his head down hard against the bench surface.

REECE: Only when it suits you 'ey? Little bastard, think you can make me into a prick?

CHANTAY: Reece!

REECE: You whisper a word of this I'll shove my fist down y'fuckin' throat!

REECE lets go, grabs his bag and heads out, setting off the fire alarm as he does so. DAVID hurries back in.

DAVID: Reece! *(Sighs.)* Right you lot, you know the drill. Out onto the playing field, far end please.

The pupils scrape their chairs and clatter out of the lab.
Only KYLE is left, the bell continues to ring.

DAVID: Some people can't take a joke.

KYLE: What d'y'do that for?

DAVID: I didn't intend it for Reece, Kyle. I didn't
think it would/

KYLE: Y'didn't, did you. Y'didn't think about wha'
might 'appen after? Y'didn't think about every
possible outcome?

DAVID: Did he have a go at you Kyle?

KYLE: Thas not the point.

DAVID: Because if he did, I'll come down on him like
a/

KYLE: I don't want y't'back me up! I don't want
y'protection, or y'friendship. I don't even want
y't'like me.

DAVID: I don't understand.

KYLE: Thas all I wanted.

KYLE grabs his bags and leaves. DAVID stands, confused.
He drinks the rest of his coffee and notices the bottom of
his cup. He tips the samples out onto the desk. He falters,
holding the desk. The alarm distorts/fades.

SCENE 5

MRS. JONES's office, tidier, but still papers piled on her desk.
DAVID and MRS. JONES, she sits and marks things off on a
sheet of paper.

MRS. JONES: Do you have any unexplained aches or
    pains?

DAVID: No.

MRS. JONES: How's your concentration?

DAVID: Fine.

MRS. JONES: Do you have a lack of energy?

DAVID: No more than usual.

MRS. JONES: So you do.

DAVID: Look Kathy, I thought we were here to talk
    about Reece.

MRS. JONES: This is something we have to do David.
    Please. Are you getting enough sleep?

DAVID: I'm usually in bed by eleven, unless it's a
    clear night.

MRS. JONES: And do you sleep all the way through?

DAVID: Sometimes.

MRS. JONES: Do you feel irritable, frustrated or
    restless?

DAVID: Right now?

MRS. JONES: Please, David.

DAVID: Sometimes.

MRS. JONES: Do you have feelings of worthlessness?

DAVID: I...no.

MRS. JONES: And finally, do you spend a lot of time thinking about death and suicide?

DAVID: Of course not!

MRS. JONES: Lovely! All done, and I'm glad to say you passed with flying colours!

DAVID: Marvellous.

MRS. JONES: Now David, this is something you agreed on when you came back to work.

DAVID: But is now the best / time?

MRS. JONES: We have to make sure you're coping.

DAVID: And as you say, I 'passed'...now, can we please talk about/

MRS. JONES: Reece, yes. What did your doctor say?

DAVID: My GP? Well from preliminary checks, no long-term damage / thankfully.

MRS. JONES: That is fantastic news! You must be over the moon. Not literally, of course.

DAVID: I'm meant to be happy? The boy tried to poison me.

MRS. JONES: We're not taking this matter lightly David, and we're about out of options with Reece...however first things first *(Quietly.)* and remember this issue is much more pressing and highly sensitive as there is a parent involved, so just keep your cool please David. *(Off.)* You can come in now Kyle!

KYLE enters. KATHY points to a chair next to DAVID for him to sit, she reads from a several pieces of lined paper.

MRS. JONES: Kyle, when I asked for an explanation, I didn't mean an essay on metaphysics.

KYLE: It's Quantum Mechanics Miss, and y'said include all the details.

MRS. JONES: About this particular incident Kyle, not *everything.* *(She reads.)* I'm confused, so there's a cat inside a box with some poison?

DAVID: It's a bit more complicated than that.

MRS. JONES: Well someone's going to have to explain.

DAVID: In the original experiment, which was meant to be hypothetical anyway, the release of the poison is triggered when a piece of radioactive material decays.

KYLE: I didn't 'ave any radioactive material did I.

DAVID: Probably because it was sat at the bottom of my coffee cup.

MRS. JONES: Mr. Milford, one thing at a time. Please. Kyle's mother is very upset. She wants something

done, and believes you're to blame. Now if it is
you filling Kyle's head with this rubbish/

KYLE: It's not rubbish.

MRS. JONES: No, but it is dangerous Kyle. I mean this
time it was just your cat. I had a dead frog in my
bin from an earlier experiment, so it seems your
subjects are getting bigger and bigger. So what
about the next time? A dog? A horse? A person
maybe?

KYLE: I didn't know what would happen.

MRS. JONES: What did you expect? You mix rat
poison with cat food, then put it in a room with
that poor creature and lock the door for the night!
Of course it was going to eat it.

KYLE: But I didn't know it f'certain!

MRS. JONES: You know I thought you were an
intelligent lad Kyle. I've got two awards here,
somewhere, for exceptional performance in both
maths and science/

DAVID: The whole point Kyle was the cat can't
interfere with the poison mechanism. The
experiment is not *about* the cat. We discussed
this, it's the decay of the radioactive material that
determines the release/

KYLE: I didn't 'ave any radioactive material did I!

DAVID: You saw Reece put those samples in my
coffee, and still you decided to say nothing.

KYLE: Maybe cos I know what happens if you interfere.

DAVID: Not even when he's trying to put my life in danger?

MRS. JONES: Mr. Milford/

KYLE: You did that when y'played that stupid joke on 'im.

DAVID: That was harmless! I'd expect you, of all people, to understand / the difference.

MRS. JONES: David! We're dealing with Reece as a separate issue. At the moment I've got a dead cat on my hands and someone needs to take the fall!

Pause.

MRS. JONES: Now I understand that Kyle was to come to your house so that he could have a look at your telescope thing/

DAVID: Observatory.

MRS. JONES: Whatever. That's not going to be happening anymore.

KYLE: But Miss/

MRS. JONES: Direct orders from your mother.

DAVID: *(Pause.)* I think it's for the best Kyle.

MRS. JONES: And when it comes to your home-made practicals, I suggest you get yourself a chemistry set.

DAVID: Mrs. Jones is right. You're not responsible enough to carry out your own experiments.

MRS. JONES: Thank you David. Now I understand that you're struggling at home right now Kyle/

KYLE: No y'don't!

MRS. JONES: But I have to suggest that you find a *healthier* outlet for your curiosities...now wait outside for me please.

KYLE goes.

MRS. JONES: This experiment, you tell me it's not on the syllabus.

DAVID: No but if a pupil has an inquiring mind Kathy, then it's my duty as a teacher to/

MRS. JONES: Duty, yes, but it's a little advanced for him isn't it, all this nuclear physics?

DAVID: Q1, the very first teaching standard, is to have high expectations from your learners/

MRS. JONES: But the safety and welfare of our learners is paramount, above any of your teaching standards! *(Pause.)* It's not your fault David.

DAVID: I'm perfectly aware of that.

MRS. JONES: But you have to understand how much influence you have over these young souls, and if you hadn't put ideas about this ridiculous cat-murdering experiment into his fragile little mind then he wouldn't have done it now, would he?...

now I don't think we're going to have a court case on our hands, but you're going to have to be very careful about your relationship with Kyle from now on.

DAVID: What about Reece?

MRS. JONES: Yes, Reece, now this is a very serious issue. We can't have pupils poisoning the staff now can we. But Reece's behaviour isn't just targeted at you, we've got a backlog of incidents and misdemeanours/

DAVID: Misdemeanour!

MRS. JONES: You don't need to raise your voice to me David. As I said, we've decided to take some quite radical steps in order to deal with Reece. In the meantime if you could try and keep radioactive stuff, or any other potentially harmful materials, out of arms reach then we can avoid problems like these, yes?

DAVID goes to leave.

MRS. JONES: And David, we are concerned about you as well.

DAVID: Concerned?

MRS. JONES: We feel you may not be settling back in quite as well as you should?

DAVID: Truthfully? It's not been easy, and with these recent events...I just don't feel I have the control that I used to.

MRS. JONES: Maybe I was a little critical in my last lesson observation, the kids seem to be having fun/

DAVID: You said they were 'unruly'.

MRS. JONES: Well maybe a little, but engaged none the less.

DAVID: You said 'bored'.

MRS. JONES: Yes, well, never mind that observation/

DAVID: I think you might be right.

MRS. JONES: God, what do I know!? It's the real inspectors that will see your true qualities as a teacher. And as the Head dropped the bombshell in briefing this morning, we're bound to have them in before the end of term, which gives us at best a month. So if you need to take some time off, sooner rather than later, eh.

DAVID: Sooner?

MRS. JONES: Well we really can't afford to have supply in when the inspectors are walking around. God, supply, David! You have more control than supply, you must see that?

DAVID: That's very...thanks.

MRS. JONES: The offer's there if you want to take it.

DAVID: I'll think about it.

MRS. JONES: Don't think about it too much though, nothing's worth dwelling on.

DAVID leaves, passing REECE, CHANTAY and KYLE by the door.

MRS. JONES: Right you three, in you come please.

They enter. CHANTAY messing with her phone

REECE: Can I 'ave sweet Miss?

MRS. JONES: They're only for pupils that have earned them Reece.

REECE: I've earned it Miss, y'not seen me on the pitch? I got bare skills.

MRS. JONES: I'm afraid that's just not going to cut it.

REECE: Why is it all the Maths and English geeks get a sweet but I never do?

MRS. JONES: Maybe because they don't try and poison their teachers Reece.

REECE: Dunno what you're on about.

MRS. JONES: Chantay, did you see anything?

CHANTAY: Nah Miss, was checkin' me messages.

MRS. JONES: *(Sighs.)* Kyle? This is the last time I'm going to ask you. Did you witness anyone putting anything into Mr. Milford's drink?

KYLE doesn't respond.

REECE: She's askin' you a question/

MRS. JONES: Alright Reece, I'll deal with this thank you. Kyle?

KYLE: What?

MRS. JONES: You need to tell me the truth now.

KYLE: I didn't see nothin'.

MRS. JONES: The truth please Kyle.

KYLE: That's it Miss, I didn't see nothin'.

REECE: *(Getting up.)* Can I go then Miss?

MRS. JONES: Er you're not going anywhere Reece. This is by no means an isolated incident, and there's no way we can go on like this.

REECE: He said he didn't see nothin'!

MRS. JONES: Just sit down! And put that thing away *now* Chantay!

They comply.

MRS. JONES: How many times have you been in my office this week already Reece?

REECE: What can I say, I like y'Miss.

MRS. JONES: That's flattering Reece, but we both know that's not the reason.

REECE: Suit y'self, I don't like y'then.

MRS. JONES: And Chantay, your levels and grades have been dropping steadily since you came into year ten.

CHANTAY: Well what is it Miss, levels or grades? Y'know what I mean? We were doin' levels up

to year nine, now it's year ten we're doin' grades.
Can't keep up.

MRS. JONES: Again Chantay, I find that hard to
swallow.

REECE: *(Snorts.)* Swallow.

She glares at REECE, he stops sniggering.

MRS. JONES: It seems that both of you are finding it
hard to work in a group, so/

The phone rings on her desk, she answers.

MRS. JONES: Hello?...*(Sighs.)*...OK, which way was
she heading...how long ago?...alright I'll try and
find her...*(She hangs up.)*...just wait here a minute
please.

REECE: Got nowhere else t'be Miss.

She goes.

CHANTAY: Tart.

REECE: I think she's fit.

CHANTAY: You seen 'ow short she wears her dresses,
she looks like a whore. Then she's got the cheek to
tell me I'm wearing too much make-up!

REECE: I think she looks good.

CHANTAY: Stuff you Reece.

REECE: I'd stuff 'er.

CHANTAY: You'd stuff anythin'.

REECE: Thas why I'm going out with you.

CHANTAY: Thas why I don't give out.

REECE: *(Frustrated.)* Slag.

CHANTAY: Y'pathetic.

REECE looks for the sweets.

REECE: Know she keeps 'em in 'ere somewhere, tight cow.

CHANTAY: She's got Maoams as well, they're my favourite.

REECE: Nah mate, Chupa Chups all the way, cherry flavoured.

KYLE: Apple.

REECE: Y'what?

KYLE: Apple's the best flavour.

REECE: Gay.

CHANTAY: I'm with you on that one Kyle, apple's lovely.

REECE: Make y'self useful retard, go on lookout.

KYLE stands in the doorway, watching the corridor outside.

REECE: Where are these bastard sweets!

The phone rings. They all freeze. It rings out. They continue searching.

KYLE: You had a look under that tea cosy on her desk?

REECE lifts it up to reveal a jar full of sweets.

REECE: You little beauty!

CHANTAY: Nice one Kyle.

REECE: *(Grabs a handful.)* Get in!

CHANTAY: Oi, not so many.

REECE: Who you, my mom?

CHANTAY: Y'don't want her to notice. God you'd be a crap thief.

REECE: Yeah? Y'ever jacked a car?

CHANTAY: That wasn't even you, that was y'brother.

REECE: I was there when he done it.

CHANTAY: Don't lie, you were nine.

REECE: I rode shotgun!

CHANTAY: You were watching Spongebob Squarepants.

REECE: Shut y'face...Kyle, my man, y'got an Xbox?

KYLE: Yeah.

REECE: Y'live?

KYLE: Course.

REECE: I'll 'ave to give you my tag later, we can link up, kick some ass.

KYLE: Nice one.

CHANTAY: God, not another one, 'Xbox this, Playstation that'. They should just plug you in and forget about you.

KYLE: You can talk, your 'and's glued to that phone.

CHANTAY: Not gamin' though am I.

KYLE: Y'finished y'documentary yet?

CHANTAY: And sent it to 'im.

KYLE: What did 'e say?

CHANTAY: Dunno, haven't 'eard back. Been days now.

KYLE: Bet 'e loves it.

CHANTAY: Worried, y'know? What if somethin' 'appened to 'im. What if 'e was too busy watchin' my film and somethin' 'appened?

KYLE: I'm sure 'e's OK Chantay.

REECE: Oi, stop y'chat a minute.

REECE is holding a piece of paper that he's picked up from the top of the pile on MRS. JONES's desk.

REECE: You've gotta check this out.

KYLE: What is it?

REECE: It's about Mr. Milford.

CHANTAY: Who?

KYLE: Science teacher.

REECE: Christ Chantay, he's the reason we're in 'ere.

CHANTAY: Not bothered.

REECE: *(Reading.)* Me...mo?

He gives it to KYLE.

CHANTAY: Whas it say?

KYLE: It's a medical form...leave of absence...'for depression...brought on by work related stress.'

REECE: Y'jokin'.

KYLE: It's a review form.

REECE: That's why 'e was off all that time, remember?

CHANTAY shrugs.

REECE: Yeah you do, remember we had a supply teacher in science for ages...before Christmas?

CHANTAY: Oh yeah.

REECE: Lyin' bastard said he had to look after his sick wife!

CHANTAY: Don't be nasty Reece, my aunty had depression.

REECE: Oh how sad, I feel a bit pissed off, I want to kill myself, boo-hoo... Get a life!

CHANTAY: Reece, it's private, you shouldn't even be looking at it.

REECE: Hey, I was in 'ere, it's on Mrs. Jones desk. I can't help it if it fell into my 'ands.

CHANTAY: Yeah but you can't tell anyone else.

REECE grins

CHANTAY: Reece!

KYLE: *(Lookout.)* Mrs. Jones!

They resume their positions, REECE drops the memo on the floor. MRS. JONES enters.

MRS. JONES: Sorry about that...now/

REECE: Can I have a sweet Miss?

MRS. JONES: Oh God, if it shuts you up!

She takes a sweet from her jar.

REECE: Nah, nah, not that one. Cherry flavoured.

She changes it and hands it over.

MRS. JONES: Now, where were we?

CHANTAY: You were talkin' about how we were finding it 'ard to work in a group Miss.

MRS. JONES: Oh yes, so the Headmaster and myself have been talking and we've decided to send you on a team-building exercise. Now it will be during school time/

REECE: Yes!

MRS. JONES: Don't get too excited Reece, you're going to have to catch up with any work that you miss.

CHANTAY: Where we goin'?

MRS. JONES: Now that *is* quite exciting, you'll be going for a day of abseiling.

REECE/CHANTAY: Yes!

REECE: Whas that?

CHANTAY: It's where you're on a rope and y'go down the side of a mountain.

REECE: Ah yes!

MRS. JONES: Now, this is meant to be a team-building exercise, not just some doss. The gentleman running the day is an ex-army officer, and he won't stand for any messing around! You'll be responsible for checking and carrying equipment/

REECE: Sabotage!

MRS. JONES: No Reece. You'll be part of a bigger group, so you've got to look out for everyone, as well as each other, and yourselves.

REECE: Don't worry Miss, I'll look after my girl.

MRS. JONES: And if there's any monkey business/

REECE: Dur, we're on ropes.

MRS. JONES: If there's any fooling around, you'll be straight back here and you'll have all privileges taken away from you quicker than you can say 'that's not fair.'...However, if you can show that you can work effectively and responsibly in a team, then you might even be invited back.

REECE: Yes Miss, Boss, Sir!

CHANTAY: Thanks Miss.

MRS. JONES: Now get yourselves back to class *(REECE is off.)* and I *do not* want to see you back in here anytime soon!

CHANTAY: I like y'dress Miss.

MRS. JONES: Thank you Chantay, now off you go.

She leaves.

MRS. JONES: You too Kyle.

KYLE: You said you 'ad some awards for me Miss.

MRS. JONES: Of course, it's a great achievement Kyle and *(Digging it out.)* there are your certificates.

He lingers.

MRS. JONES: Is there anything else Kyle?

KYLE: Yeah, er, no...sorry Miss, Chantay and Reece goin' abseiling, as punishment?

MRS. JONES: I know it seems strange Kyle, but Reece and Chantay have got...well, they're different. And we need an alternative approach to deal with that sometimes.

KYLE: And y'think that's fair?

MRS. JONES: Look, you just keep your head down. You're doing fantastically well, which is why you've been rewarded.

KYLE: *(Waving certificate.)* Great.

MRS. JONES: Good lad, now let's not see *you* slipping OK?

He's going to say something, but doesn't and leaves. KATHY sighs and slumps on her chair. She notices the piece of paper on the floor, the memo about DAVID. She picks it up and looks at it

SCENE 6

Playground. REECE, KYLE and CHANTAY are sitting on a rail. They're eating sandwiches, crisps etc. REECE has his arm around CHANTAY's shoulder.

REECE: I flayed yo ass on Call of Duty last night, nang!

KYLE: Then you woke up, yeah?

REECE: Whas that?

KYLE: You were dreamin', right?

REECE: The only thing I dream about is this beautiful lady.

CHANTAY: Dream on.

REECE: Not when I got the real thing.

They snog and stay linked.

CHANTAY: Ham and pickle, yum.

REECE: Wanna play sandwiches?

CHANTAY: Don't get frisky.

REECE: I could be the meat, you could be the bread.

CHANTAY: Then we're gonna need another slice...
Kyle?

REECE: What? You, me and...urgh, get off me slag!

CHANTAY: Fine, just me and you then Kyle yeah?

REECE: Just try it.

CHANTAY: And what?

Pause. REECE shouts to someone in the playground.

REECE: Oi Fin...Oi four eyes! Y'dad's a gimp!

REECE chucks a bit of sandwich crust at him.

REECE: We gave them Yanks a right thrashin' last
night, ain't that right Kyle.

KYLE: Proper...they did sound about eight years old
though.

REECE: Remember the bunker?

KYLE: Sweet.

REECE: One of us snipin'.

KYLE: One coverin' the door.

REECE: Just pickin' em off... Nang!

They're side by side, KYLE low, REECE high, simulating shooting. CHANTAY films on her mobile.

KYLE: No idea where we were. Pure camouflage.

REECE: Dunno what t'look for.

REECE now positions himself opposite KYLE

REECE: Me, I just wait. It's a waitin' game. Use the sight to recon the area, just waitin' for the light to catch the front of y'scope then...blam!

Slow motion. REECE uses his finger to trace the path of the bullet, it hits KYLE between the eyes, who then falls onto his back.

CHANTAY: Y'look like a right pair of twats.

REECE: You do.

CHANTAY: I'm gonna bounce, find someone my own age.

REECE: Babe?

CHANTAY: Y'pissin' about like it's some kinda game!

REECE: Easy.

KYLE: You 'eard from 'im Chantay?

CHANTAY: We got to Skype last night but our webcam's well dodgy, loads of lag, so the image was dead jumpy. Doesn't 'elp, makes y'think there's bombs goin' off all the time.

KYLE: 'Ow's he doin'?

CHANTAY: Sprained 'is ankle.

REECE: Muppet.

CHANTAY: 'E was meant to be out on early patrol, jumps out of bed so eager 'e twists 'is ankle, 'ad to stay behind. Find out later in the day that a roadside bomb ripped through the patrol vehicle, killed all four of the soldiers on board... God bless my muppet brother.

REECE: I'd love to be out there, y'know. Clippin' some ragheads.

CHANTAY: Y'wouldn't last five minutes.

REECE: Y'doubt my strength?

CHANTAY: That ain't all.

CHANTAY points the camera at KYLE.

CHANTAY: Y'don't 'ave to be like 'im.

She leaves. KYLE gestures for a helping hand from REECE but he's blanked. He gets up by himself and both boys end up propped on the rail. REECE shouts off stage

REECE: Sir!... Sir!!... We got football t'nite?...yeah I've done it...I've done it!...nice one.

He waits for Sir to walk away then throws a bit of sandwich crust at him.

REECE: Nang, got 'im.

KYLE: You were miles off.

REECE: Was I askin?

Pause.

REECE: 'You wouldn't last five minutes'. I'm tellin you if I had a real gun...

KYLE: Yeah? What?

REECE: I'd take out bare people.

KYLE: Course y'would.

REECE: I would, and I'd start right 'ere.

KYLE: You're wrong in the 'ead.

REECE: Come off it, you tellin' me there ain't some teachers you'd like to see get capped?

KYLE: Serious?...nah, I ain't into that.

REECE: So you're a pussyboy?

KYLE: I ain't a pussy.

REECE: Must just be your 'air that makes you look like one, 'ere, let me fix it.

REECE gets KYLE in a headlock and ruffles his hair hard.
KYLE struggle to get free, but it's REECE that lets him go.

REECE: 'Ello, here comes one now. Though I reckon 'e'd top 'imself before I could get a look in.

DAVID enters, he's on playground duty. He looks worn. The boys back up to the rail.

DAVID: Reece...Kyle.

REECE: Sir.

DAVID: They've fired up the Hadron Collidor Kyle, the results should be pouring in soon.

KYLE: So?

REECE: Hadron wha'?

DAVID: I thought you'd be interested to know.

REECE: Oh no Sir, 'e is interested, don't read anythin' into that bored-shitless look on 'is face.

DAVID: *(Pause.)* Get yourselves away from the rail, you know the rules.

REECE: Yes Mr. Milford, sorry Sir...are we doin' a practical in Science Sir?

DAVID: Well that depends, doesn't it.

REECE: 'Ow's that Sir?

DAVID: It depends on what you do for me.

REECE: I ain't givin' you a blowjob if that's what you mean Sir.

KYLE snorts with laughter.

DAVID: Er Reece, I'll remind you that you're not to use language like that in school.

REECE: Sorry Sir, slip of the tongue. *(Slurps.)*

DAVID: Just watch yourselves, both of you.

REECE: Sir.

DAVID walks off. REECE pelts a bit of crust at him, immediately acting nonchalant. DAVID comes back on holding the piece of crust.

DAVID: Alright, which one of you was it?

REECE: Sir?

DAVID: Which one of you threw this at me?

REECE: I dunno what you're on about Sir.

DAVID: I know it was one of you so *which one was it?*

REECE: I haven't got a sandwich Sir.

KYLE is still eating his. DAVID looks at him

KYLE: What?... It wasn't me.

DAVID: Detention Kyle.

KYLE: Ey, I 'aven't chucked nothin'!

DAVID: Don't you shout at me!

KYLE: But y'can't just/

DAVID: I really don't know what's happened to you Kyle, you used to be such a nice lad.

KYLE: Yeah, well you've always been a prick.

DAVID: Right! That's an hour detention with me, and a Senior Management detention as well. You don't swear at staff Kyle! Am I understood?!

KYLE stares at him.

DAVID: You can pick your slips up at the end of the day. If I don't see you then, you'll be getting another one.

DAVID exits. KYLE is fuming.

KYLE: *(To REECE.)* Whatcha do that for?!

REECE: Easy brother.

KYLE: It's your fault!

REECE: Ey, I didn't give you the detentions.

KYLE: What a complete bastard!

REECE: Kyle, don't get mad...

REECE reaches into his bag and takes out a spray paint can, he gives it to KYLE.

REECE: He's got a white Astra, number plate starts with a W.

KYLE shakes the can, pops the lid.

SCENE 7

A science lab, it is a mess. As in Scene 4, only part of the lab is represented. There is a full class, the lesson is a lot more unsettled than the lesson in Scene 4.

In the lab there are trays of equipment; tripods, gauzes, crucibles, jars of copper oxide/carbon powder. Bunsen burners are set up on the benches. DAVID looks dishevelled, he is waiting anxiously at the door, looking at his watch.

DAVID: You're late!

REECE: *(Off.)* Bell's only just gone.

DAVID: Yes, and you're meant to be here before the bell or bang on the bell, certainly not after it. That bell is an indicator for me to start the lesson, not for you to decide to make your way here.

REECE: *(Off.)* Take a pill Sir.

DAVID: I beg your pardon! Get inside now!

REECE and CHANTAY traipse in. CHANTAY intermittently films the events of the lessons on her mobile.

DAVID: I'm still waiting for a reason.

REECE: Sorry Sir, got kept behind at registration.

DAVID: And what's your excuse Chantay?

CHANTAY: Ain't got one.

DAVID: Well that's not good enough. You can give me five minutes at the end of the lesson.

CHANTAY: Y'what?! What about Reece?

REECE: Hey, I couldn't help it.

DAVID: Bags and coats at the back of the class, quickly.

REECE: We doin' a practical Sir?

DAVID: What does it look like to you Reece?

REECE: Bunsen Burners?

DAVID: We will need to use the gas, yes but/

REECE: Sweet!

DAVID: But the first sign of inappropriate behaviour and we'll put away the practical and get out the worksheets.

REECE: Swear I'll be good Sir.

DAVID: Well, we'll see. *(Addressing class.)* Right, so first you'll need to know what you're doing as this can be a fun but quite a dangerous experiment/

REECE: Yeah right.

DAVID: because of the kinds of temperatures we're dealing with. So what's the first thing we have to remember? Chantay?

CHANTAY: *(Shrugs.)* Brush y'teeth?

DAVID: No Chantay, goggles! Now this is a reduction, oxidation experiment, or a displacement reaction/

KYLE wanders in.

DAVID: Right young man, and what's your excuse?

KYLE: *(Mutters.)* What's yours.

DAVID: Chantay's already got five minutes, so you can give me ten minutes at the end of the lesson.

KYLE: Whatever.

DAVID: Let's make it the whole of break then shall we.

REECE: Ah come on Sir, cut 'im some slack. 'e 'ad t'go see 'is Art teacher. 'e gets well into his Art Sir, especially 'is *painting.* Y'know what I mean Sir?

REECE makes the sound of a spray can. DAVID is thrown.

DAVID: Coat and bag at the back Kyle, and quickly, you've wasted enough of my time.

KYLE smirks with REECE, they bump fists as KYLE passes him.

DAVID: Quickly Kyle! *(To all.)* Now I've promised myself that I'm not going to let you ruin today's lesson, so I'm damned if I'm going to let you behave in this fashion! *(Calming himself.)* Right, now, two different chemicals, one is a compound called copper oxide. So what is a compound?

REECE: Ain't it like a lockdown Sir?

DAVID: A lockdown?

REECE: Y'know, prison.

DAVID: Not in this case Reece. A compound is two or more elements that are chemically bonded. So what two elements are in copper oxide do you think?

CHANTAY: What's an element Sir?

DAVID: Well, in the other jar we have carbon which is an example of an element. An element is something that exists on its own, in its simplest form, so this is just carbon.

CHANTAY: They both look the same to me Sir.

DAVID: They're both black powders that's right Chantay, but believe me, they're very different... So what do you think is in copper oxide? Kyle?

KYLE: Dunno.

DAVID: I don't believe you Kyle.

KYLE: Nothin' I can do about that.

DAVID: Come on, the clue is in the name.

REECE: Is it copper Sir?

DAVID: Finally! Well done Reece, that's right, there is copper in it. What about the oxide part? Listen to the start of the word, ox...what element starts with ox...? ox...? Kyle?

KYLE: Why d'y'keep askin' me?

DAVID: Because I know you know the answer Kyle, this is basic stuff!

KYLE: So ask someone else then!

REECE: Is it oxide sir?

DAVID: Close Reece, it's oxygen. Right, now, we're going to be mixing these two chemicals together, carbon and copper oxide, then heating them with a roaring blue flame. That's the hottest Bunsen flame.

REECE: Come on!

DAVID: What you should see happen is quite remarkable... *(Off.)* Jordan, stop talking...the carbon is going to bond with the oxygen in the copper oxide. It's going to *displace* the oxygen from the copper oxide...Jordan!...and the carbon is going to become *oxidised*, forming what gas?... Come on, we breathe it out all the time...

REECE: Oxygen?

DAVID: No Reece.

CHANTAY: *(Head on desk.)* Carbon dioxide.

DAVID: Excellent Chantay! So in effect the carbon is going to 'steal' the oxygen from the copper oxide, because it is more reactive than the copper. So if it takes the oxygen away from the copper oxide, what are we going to be left with?

REECE: Carbon dioxide!

DAVID: Copper...so what you should see is these two black powders turn into...this stuff.

He holds up a jar of Copper clippings.

DAVID: Alright, so, take a few spatulas of each powder. Mix them carefully in the crucible, place them on top of the tripod and gauze, and then heat them with the Bunsen flame from underneath...got it?

ALL: Yes sir!

They start to grab equipment, REECE is being particularly heavy handed.

DAVID: Don't forget your goggles!

They set up. KYLE reluctantly, but correctly, sets up. REECE puts three pairs of goggles on his face. CHANTAY puts some spatulas of Copper Oxide in her crucible and starts playing with it with her finger, this is as far as she gets with the experiment.

CHANTAY: It's dead soft this stuff, ain't it Sir.

DAVID: It's a very fine powder, yes Chantay. Can you stop messing with it and get on with what I've asked you to do.

REECE: Can we take it home when we've finished Sir?

DAVID: Unfortunately not Reece, and you're only meant to wear *one* pair of goggles. Take them off!

He doesn't.

CHANTAY: What are we meant to get from this Sir?

DAVID: Well Chantay, it's one way that we can get copper from the ground, as it exists in the Earth's crust as copper oxide. And we use copper in so many things, can you think of any?

CHANTAY shrugs.

DAVID: Well, what about the coins in your pocket?

CHANTAY: How do you know what I've got in my pocket?

REECE starts banging a tripod against the desk.

DAVID: I'm just saying, ones and two pences are mostly copper...and electrical wiring, pots and pans, because it's such a good conductor of both electricity and heat...Reece, stop it or you'll be out!

He doesn't.

CHANTAY: It's a metal ain't it, copper?

DAVID: That's right *(Off.)* Emily, put that make-up away!

CHANTAY: So is it used in like bullets and stuff?

DAVID: No, it's quite malleable and ductile. Which means it can be hammered into sheets or drawn into wires, like electrical wires.

CHANTAY: So it's not used in like tanks, or armoured vehicles.

DAVID: No, it's quite soft...Reece!

REECE: What!

DAVID: Right, that's it! Get out...now! Put that down, takes those goggles off and get out!

REECE: I wasn't doin' nothin'!

DAVID: GET OUT!

REECE: Alright, alright, where am I meant to go?

DAVID: I don't care, just get outside.

REECE: Don't commit suicide, Emo.

REECE leaves. DAVID tries to compose himself.

DAVID: Right, the rest of you, are we ready to turn on the gas?...OK, make sure all taps are off, otherwise I can't turn it on from mains supply. So taps at right angles to the nozzle?...OK.

He turns a key on a panel that controls gas/water/electricity by his desk. A few moments, an alarm sounds.

DAVID: Someone hasn't turned off their tap, Chantay?

CHANTAY: Check it Sir, right angles yeah?

DAVID: Kyle?

No response. DAVID strides up to him.

DAVID: What did I say Kyle? What did I say?!

KYLE: Y'spittin' in my face!

DAVID: Right angles! You haven't forgotten what a right angle is have you Kyle?!

DAVID turns off his tap.

DAVID: Right, and again.

He turns the key, this time no alarm. The gas is on.

DAVID: OK, so, matches and splints are in the trays.
Don't light your Bunsen with a match. Use the
length of the splint please! And make sure the air
holes are fully closed. I want yellow flames to start
with!

MRS. JONES enters with REECE.

MRS. JONES: Mr. Milford can I have a word? Go and
sit yourself down Reece.

DAVID: I sent him out Mrs. Jones, for very good
reason.

MRS. JONES: I'm sure you did Mr. Milford and we've
been having a good talk outside, haven't we Reece.

REECE: Yes Miss.

MRS. JONES: Now Reece knows that he's done
something wrong.

DAVID: Damn right, he doesn't know how to behave
safely and responsibly during a practical!

MRS. JONES: Yes, but he's sorry for his behaviour and
would like to apologise, isn't that right Reece.

REECE: Thas right Miss.

MRS. JONES: Well go on then.

REECE: Sorry Sir.

DAVID: I'm afraid it's too late Reece.

REECE: Come off it, I wasn't the only one/

MRS. JONES: Reece.

REECE: Yeah but 'ow can he/

MRS. JONES: Reece!

REECE: Bumbaclart.

MRS. JONES takes DAVID to one side.

MRS. JONES: David, I understand the problems you're having with Reece/

DAVID: That's not the point Kathy. He's behaving in a dangerous manner in the lab, which means he can't be part of the practical.

MRS. JONES: So give him a worksheet...look, the inspectors are having a tour of the school *as we speak.* Now we can't have naughty children stood out in the corridors with such important visitors wandering around.

DAVID: Well can't he go to the student review centre with you?

MRS. JONES: *(Agitated.)* You know I'm busy with the inspectors, as are most of Senior Management. God David, can you just for once be a team player, yes?

DAVID: *(Pause.)* Alright...Reece! Get your book and come and sit here, you've got a thousand unfinished worksheets stuck in there that you can be getting on with...hurry up!

He does so, deliberately slowly.

MRS. JONES: Thank you, it won't be forgotten...and if you could tuck your shirt in David, you look like a scruff.

She leaves. The rest of the class jeer and laugh at her last comment as DAVID tucks in his shirt.

DAVID: That's enough!

DAVID tries one more time to snap into a positive mood. CHANTAY is messing with her phone.

DAVID: Right, how are the rest of us getting along... Chantay, you still haven't set up your tripod and gauze!...Kyle! Oh, you've made a start, good lad.

REECE: Which worksheet d'y'want me to do Sir?

DAVID: I don't care Reece, just do one of them and stop talking.

REECE: Yeah but it's good t'talk Sir, get things off y'chest like.

DAVID: I'm not interested Reece.

REECE: See that's y'problem Sir, y'keep it all bottled up...no wonder y'get depressed.

DAVID: What was that?

REECE: I said no wonder you get depressed Sir, if y'don't talk about y'problems, y'know.

DAVID: I have no idea what you're talking about Reece.

REECE: Ah come on Sir, might not be good at Science but I ain't stupid. Everyone knows you were off with depression, all that crap about 'olidays and y'wife's illness. You was depressed Sir.

DAVID: Who have you been talking to?

REECE: Everyone knows Sir. It's weak really, couldn't face the world, is that what it was? All too much for ya? Boo-hoo, gonna slit me wrists?

DAVID: Shut your mouth Reece.

REECE: Or what, y'gonna cry?

DAVID: I'm warning you Reece, shut your mouth.

REECE: I'm the least of your worries *David.*

REECE gestures. Behind DAVID, KYLE is burning some paper, probably his exercise book, in the Bunsen flame. DAVID storms up to him and snatches it away, stamping it out on the floor. He explodes.

DAVID: Of all the ignorant...you stupid boy! Just what do you think you're playing at?!

KYLE: Fuck off.

DAVID: Fuck off?... Fuck off?! I'll teach you to fuck off!

DAVID grabs him by the collar and drags him into the storeroom.

KYLE: Get off me y'twat, get off me!

They disappear and the door slams. REECE bolts to it and peers through the little window in the door

REECE: Oh shit!...Chantay, come look...Chantay!

CHANTAY wanders over filming on her phone, she reaches the window and looks inside. She recoils, backing away. She drops the phone and runs out into the corridor.

SCENE 8

The prep room, as we left DAVID and KATHY in Scene 1.

MRS. JONES: What has God got to do with this?

DAVID: That's what they call it, the Higgs boson. The God particle, the hole in the jigsaw...but if it can explain it all, add that missing piece to the Grand Unified Theory, creating a Theory of Everything... why are there still gaps?

MRS. JONES: You can't explain everything. It's impossible.

DAVID: Everything is possible, but with a mind peppered by black holes?

MRS. JONES: What do you remember?

DAVID: There's no escape.

MRS. JONES: From this morning.

DAVID: Watching a black sunrise over an event horizon.

MRS. JONES: What *happened* David?

DAVID: Destined to fall in, watching a black sun drop below the event horizon.

MRS. JONES: David?

DAVID: There was an old man of Wight,
Who travelled much faster than light,
He departed one day, in a relative way,
And arrived on the previous night.

MRS. JONES: The pupils are telling me...what they're telling me, I just can't believe.

DAVID: This is not me, it's not me, not me.

MRS. JONES: Kyle is...he's badly hurt. His head, they're saying you hit him.

DAVID: If you could go back, Kathy. If you could only go back and change things. That's all he wanted, to go back, change things.

MRS. JONES: They say you used a weapon.

DAVID: Of course you've got to understand the basics before you can make that leap.

MRS. JONES: There's blood everywhere.

DAVID: But he didn't have the patience, you've got to have patience!

MRS. JONES: He's not responding David.

DAVID: I'd like to go home now.

MRS. JONES: The paramedics are with him as we speak.

DAVID: I want to go home to my wife and children.

MRS. JONES: The police will need to talk to you.

DAVID: I need to go back, make it all better.

MRS. JONES: You can't go back David.

DAVID: It is possible, they've done it Kathy. Those boys at CERN. We can go back, we can fix this.

MRS. JONES: David?

He gets up and walks to the 'floating hammer'. KATHY tenses. He taps the ruler and the mechanism starts to rock.

DAVID: You can see it, but you don't believe it. It's happening, but you know it shouldn't be. I used to be excited by that idea, now it just scares me.

MRS. JONES: There's nothing to be afraid of, no one wants to hurt you.

DAVID: I've got a metallic taste in my mouth.

Pause.

DAVID: What should I do now?

MRS. JONES: Someone will be along shortly.

DAVID: So we just wait?

MRS. JONES: What are we going to tell them?

DAVID: Everything.

Pause.

DAVID: I think I'll spend this evening in the observatory. Yes. Track those restless stars, put them at ease. Then bed. Things will look better in the morning. They always do.

Lights fade until only the 'floating hammer' is visible.